ARCHITECTURE OF THAILAND

PROJECT MANAGER
Ekanong Sookasem

EDITORIAL TEAM – A49
Ekanong Sookasem
Suluck Visavapattamawon
Chana Sumpalung

ADVISORS
Professor M. R. Nengnoi Suksri
Chulalongkorn University

Professor Khaisang Sukhavadhana
Chulalongkorn University

Professor Ornsiri Panin
Silpakorn University

Professor Pussadee Tiptus
Chulalongkorn University

Associate Professor Lersom Sthapitanonda
Chulalongkorn University

Associate Professor Dr Santi Chantavilasvong
Chulalongkorn University

Assistant Professor Dr M. L. Piyalada Devakula Thaveeprungsriporn
Chulalongkorn University

Group Captain Arvuth Ngoenchuklin
Ministry of Culture

Wongchat Chatrakul Na Ayuddaya
Ministry of Culture

Ronarit Dhanakoses
National Discovery Museum Institute

PRINCIPAL PHOTOGRAPHERS
Michael Freeman
Luca Tettoni
Robert McLeod

CONTRIBUTING PHOTOGRAPHERS
Brian Mertens
Somkid Paimpiyachat
Teerawat Winyarat
Sorawich Homsuwan

RESEARCH TRANSLATOR
Paveena Viriyaprapaikit

RESEARCH LEADERS – A49
Kiattisak Veteewootacharn
Nitis Sthapitanonda
Karnchit Punyakanok
Phaithaya Banchakitikun
Viyada Charoensook Wongwigkarn
Sawapat Chaiyarerk

RESEARCHERS – A49
Rungroj Leesinsawat
Salyawate Prasertwitayakarn
Suweenaporn Phongsopa
Tatchapon Lertwirojkul
Woranol Sattayavinij
Woraphot Linkanograt
Thiti Ophatsodsai
Methiga Tangkaewfa
Piboon Amornjiraporn
Wareeyos Waewsawangwong
Peeranu Soonthornsaratoon
Prayut Sae-Aung
Jariyawat Vaeteewootacharn
Natjaporn Kosalanun

ILLUSTRATORS
Nithi Sthapitanonda
Chanasit Chonlasuek
Narongrit Thongsang
Napat Kwanmuang
Naruporn Saowanit
Suphawat Hiranthanawiwat
Athit Limmun
Weerapon Singnoi

ILLUSTRATION CREDITS

PAGE 3: *Base of a gilded chedi, Wat Chompoo, Chiang Mai.*
PAGE 4: *Carved ventilation panel over a door, Pattani province.*
PAGE 5: *Naga eave brackets, Wat Rasisalai, Roi Et province.*
PAGE 6: *Viharn Lai Kham, Wat Phra Singh, Chiang Mai.*
PAGE 7: *Carved wood door panel, Wat Pratu Pong, Lampang.*
PAGE 8: *Gold-and-lacquer window panel, Wat Saket, Bangkok.*
PAGE 9: *Painted door panels, Wat Suthat, Bangkok.*
PAGE 248: *Ubosot, Wat Donsak, Uttaradit province.*

First published in the United Kingdom in 2006 by
Thames & Hudson Ltd, 181A High Holborn, London WC1V 7QX

www.thamesandhudson.com

First published in hardcover in the United States of Amercia in 2006 by
Thames & Hudson Inc, 500 Fifth Avenue, New York, New York 10110

thameshudsonusa.com

© 2005 Editions Didier Millet

British Library Cataloguing-in-Publication Data
A catalogue record for this book is available from the British Library

Library of Congress Catalog Number: 2005907893

ISBN-13: 978-0-500-34223-7

ISBN-10: 0-500-34223-7

Printed and bound in Singapore

The authors would like to thank the following companies for their generous support.
Raimon Land, Jim Thompson, The Siam Cement Group, King Power.

Nithi Sthapitanonda and Brian Mertens

ARCHITECTURE OF THAILAND

A Guide to Traditional and Contemporary Forms

Thames & Hudson

Contents

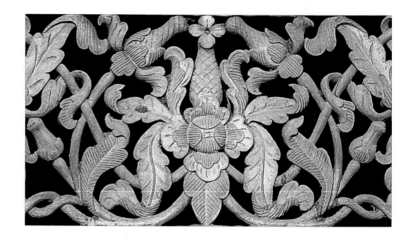

Preface

The new millennium, from the Thai point of view, is already very old. It is the 26th century of the Buddhist Era, and in Thailand, traditional architecture still plays a meaningful role. More than in most countries, architecture embodies the nation's identity. Thailand's spirituality and monarchical traditions, its agrarian roots, its rich mix of ethnic and foreign influences, can all be traced in buildings. So can the Thai sense of beauty.

That is partly why books on Thai architecture are of value. Many excellent volumes explore topics which include regional styles and genres such as houses. But there has long been a need for a closer look at architectural elements. Classical Thai buildings are entire orchestras of forms, and the melody can be hard to catch on a first listen. It helps to start by tuning in to each instrument one at a time. A temple door, for example, might be decorated to replicate the form of a whole building in miniature, with base, columns and ornamented roof all crafted in fine detail. The symbolism and sheer beauty of these elements begs a closer look. In all of world architecture, there may be no doors more delightful.

With that in mind, this book is designed for reference and inspiration, as a guide and source book. It presents a full range of architectural forms in a systematic manner, with lots of images for comparison. It is for Thais and foreigners, travellers and architecture enthusiasts.

It is also meant to help designers and architects. At a time when traditional Thai architecture is being re-explored as a tool kit for contemporary applications, we hope to suggest a sensitive approach to the past. Classical forms and elements cannot be used indiscriminately in Thailand, as some builders have discovered when their projects meet with public disapproval, even protests. Most temple and palace forms embody forms of reverence—towards religion and the monarchy.

Fluent architects are abstracting traditional forms and concepts, reinterpreting forms imaginatively while respecting the past.

We hope to inspire readers to visit more sites and to simply better appreciate the everyday architecture all around Thailand. It does not take a trip up-country to see the best of it. Bangkok has some 450 temples, but even most residents visit just a dozen in a lifetime. Happily this means city temples are oases of tranquillity.

The ever-changing collective sense of what is best and most significant in Thai architecture sometimes needs fresh inspiration. Regional architecture has been in vogue since the 1990s. We feature many beautiful Lanna temples, of course, but we want to re-emphasise central Siamese style, especially Rattanakosin architecture from the 19th and early 20th centuries. When the best of this architecture was created, primarily under royal sponsorship and supervision, it managed to be not only traditional but also innovative, even avant-garde. In this, it was part of the spirit of changing times. Siam's modernisation under kings Rama IV, Rama V and Rama VI was proclaimed in architecture, in an exuberant embrace of foreign styles and an eclectic approach towards Siam's own architectural past. European architecture was not a colonial imposition as in other Asian countries; the royals made it Thai. These pages feature many examples of this, and also cover some neglected topics such as shophouses and Islamic architecture.

Today's trend towards neo-traditional architecture has produced some fine results, but it cannot be sustained without the survival of tradition itself. Fortunately, there is growing interest in the conservation of Thailand's old buildings and traditional neighbourhoods. But there is not yet a major government-supported heritage effort. With just such an effort, Thailand's architectural heritage will survive not only in books, but as a living legacy that will enrich Thai life in the 27th century.

Acknowledgements

This book came to fruition with the help of many people and institutions who shared their expertise, images and love for architecture.

A tremendous role was played by Architects 49 and its staff. Thanks above all to project manager Ekanong Sookasem, who contributed her sharp intelligence in photo selection, research, organisation and conceptualisation. Suluck Visavapattamawon, Chana Sumpalung and Nitis Sthapitanonda were all of great help. So were Kiattisak Veteewootacharn, Piboon Amornjiraporn, Wareeyos Waewsawangwong, who focused on images and trial layouts. They, and other staff, also helped with photo shoots, research and enthusiasm.

In Singapore, EDM editor Laura Jeanne Gobal mastered the project's innumerable details and provided many fresh ideas. Designers Nelani Jinadasa and Felicia Wong always came up with inspired results.

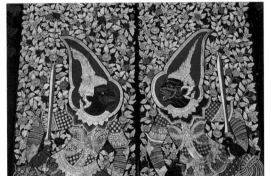

Sourcing photographs of forms and elements was a challenge we overcame thanks to photographers Michael Freeman, Luca Tettoni and Robert McLeod. Additional photos were taken by Somkid Paimpiyachat and Teerawat Winyarat for the Association of Siamese Architects under Royal Patronage, which kindly allowed us to use their inspiring shots. The National Archives offered historical images, and Chawinkorn Wongnoppasit's T. S. E. Technology Co. provided Thai motifs. We are also indebted to Nakorn Pongnoi at Rai Mae Fah Luang, artist Thawan Duchanee, and Jim Thompson House.

At the early stages, several experts helped to map out the scope of the work. Professor M. R. Nengnoi Suksri provided detailed information on the Grand Palace; Assistant Professor Dr M. L. Piyalada Thaveeprungsriporn shared research on the aesthetics of the Siamese house; Professor Ornsiri Panin advised on vernacular architecture; Professor Pussadee Tiptus informed on architecture in the Rattanakosin period; and Associate Professor Dr Santi Chantavilasvong shed light on Thai geography.

Dr Roxanna Brown of Bangkok University Museum advised on architectural ceramics. Also helpful was Group Captain Arvuth Agoenchuklin, Ministry of Culture, who gave research suggestions. Professor Khaisang Sukhavadhana discussed architectural elements.

Richard Sandler and Chalerm Saiyavuth led us to remote sites along the Chao Phraya River. Also of help were Ronarit Dhanakoses, answering queries on religious architecture, and Wongchat Chatrakul Na Ayuddaya, on decorative details. Associate Professor Dr Wiroj Srisuro and Phahonchai Premjai advised on Isaan temples. Thanks too to Paveena Viriyaprapaikit, who translated the many research documents, and Navamintr Vitayakul, who scrutinised proofs.

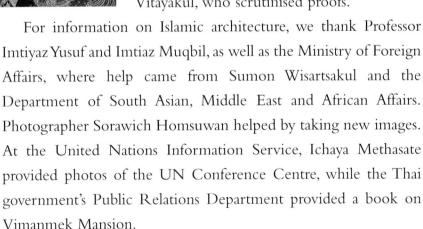

For information on Islamic architecture, we thank Professor Imtiyaz Yusuf and Imtiaz Muqbil, as well as the Ministry of Foreign Affairs, where help came from Sumon Wisartsakul and the Department of South Asian, Middle East and African Affairs. Photographer Sorawich Homsuwan helped by taking new images. At the United Nations Information Service, Ichaya Methasate provided photos of the UN Conference Centre, while the Thai government's Public Relations Department provided a book on Vimanmek Mansion.

Personal thanks to Allen and Gloria Mertens, Claudia Bieri, Dr Apichart Intravisit, Robert Halliday, Elaine Ng, Christopher Drake, Philip Cornwel-Smith, Chartvichai Promadhattavedi, Dr Anucha Thirakanont and Professor William Chapman.

An Architecture of Layers

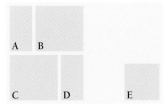

A. *One of the Monuments of the Royal Insignia in the Temple of the Emerald Buddha at the Grand Palace. Standing in a busabok throne encircled by royal parasols, the three-pronged vajra with lightning bolts represents the reign of King Rama VI.*

B. *Northern Thai layers: the quadruple Buddha image of Wat Phumin in Nan presides on a triple-tiered pedestal amid exquisite carved wood and gilded lacquer decoration.*

C. *The many tiers of this prang tower are embellished with mouldings, redentations, crockery mosaic and guardian figures that trace influences from Indian, Khmer, Chinese and Middle Eastern art.*

D. *Each of the eight prang towers at the Temple of the Emerald Buddha embodies three strata of culture. The tower is a 19th-century Thai rendition of a Khmer monumental form dating to the 12th century, based on still more ancient Khmer and Indian sikhara sanctuaries.*

E. *Thai thought has been shaped by a Hindu-Siamese treatise known as the Traiphum, which envisions time and space as layers of oceans and peaks encircling the mythical Mount Meru. This illustration appears in a 1776 manuscript version commissioned by King Taksin.*

Thailand has not one architecture, but at least three, each with regional variations. First, an everyday traditional architecture of bamboo or wooden houses on posts with prefabricated walls, steep gable roofs and an open space below the cabin. Second, a ceremonial architecture of richly ornamented temples and palaces that while distinctly Thai, subsumes influences from India, Ceylon, Burma, Cambodia, Laos, China and the West.

Third is the nation's assortment of immigrant, foreign and modern architectures in both pure and hybrid forms. These are no less important for being foreign. Chinese shophouses, for example, are the building blocks of Thai towns. The many Western-style palaces built since the mid-19th century are pillars of Thai architectural identity and royal identity.

Thailand has made the best of being situated at a geographic and cultural crossroads, and its architecture is proof of this. Religious and royal architecture in particular have evolved through a process of layering; a remarkable Thai capacity for the accretion of forms and influences over time.

This 'layering' is a form in itself, one that expresses a deeply Thai world-view shaped by a 13th-century Siamese treatise on Theravada Buddhist cosmology called the Traiphum, or The Three Worlds. This key doctrine explains time, space and human existence within a Hindu-Buddhist system of hierarchical layers. For living beings, time comprises cycles of birth and rebirth in which one hopes to attain an ever higher form of existence through the accumulation of merit by doing good deeds.

This progress through oceans of time can be plotted in space. The Traiphum diagrams the universe as a *mandala* of concentric mountains and seas surrounding a sacred hub, the mythical Himalayan abode of the gods called Mount Meru. This sacred peak is symbolised by the multi-tiered conical forms used in royal regalia such as crowns and parasols, and throughout temple and palace architecture: bases, the tops of wall columns, stupas and roof spires.

Preceding pages: The dazzling spires and multi-tiered roofs of the Grand Palace herald a traditional architecture that is richly layered in influences and forms.

1.1 The Sukhothai Era and its Origins

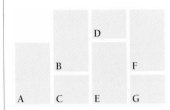

A. The lotus bud chedi form, unique to the Sukhothai civilisation, is thought to derive from the Khmer prang tower. Siamese builders revised the Khmer-Hindu predecessor with the lotus' shape and Buddhist symbolism.

B. Monumental Buddha images reveal the artistry of Sukhothai sculptors. This statue, 12.5 m tall, stands in the ruins of a mondop enclosure at Wat Saphan Hin.

C. The ground plan of the Sukhothai-era temple compound reflects the cosmological inspiration that shaped Khmer temples. The rows of pillars in this wat once supported a wooden gable roof to form an open chapel.

D. The ruins of a lotus bud chedi at Wat Mahathat, Sukhothai's key temple.

E. Towering influence: ruins of a prang sanctuary at Prasat Phnom Rung in Buri Ram province, dating from Thailand's pre-Thai Khmer era.

F. Wat Chedi Chet Thae features a lotus bud chedi surrounded by 32 smaller chedis, representing the 32 points on the compass. It stands in Sri Satchanalai, a vassal kingdom of Sukhothai, located some 50 km away.

G. Sukhothai's Wat Sri Sawai centres on three laterite prang towers dating from the 13th century. Bayon-era Khmers built it as a Hindu sanctuary, which the Siamese later transformed for Buddhist ritual.

The Thais are believed to have reached Thailand around a millennium ago, probably from ancestral homelands in southern China, spreading in a pattern of both migration and geographic extension through population growth. Among the first and most important of their many early local kingdoms was Sukhothai, established in 1238. It was absorbed by Ayutthaya in 1378, but had its own king until 1438. By weight of tradition more than unanimous scholarship, Sukhothai's name is given to the first epoch of Thai history.

Sukhothai-era houses and palaces, built of wood, have long since vanished, but temple ruins indicate a distinctive architecture. Temple halls were built with open walls, masonry columns and wooden gable roofs. Even in brick and stone, these halls featured sloping, trapezoidal uprights, a characteristically Thai geometry borrowed from houses.

Temple architecture was shaped by peoples who preceded the Thais in what is now Thailand. The influence of the Khmers, dominant there from the 9th through to the 13th centuries, shows in the Hindu cosmology of temple ground plans. The prang memorial tower and its surrounding cloisters are also Khmer-derived structures.

The key architectural influence of the Mons, dominant from the 6th to the 9th centuries, was an indirect result of the Theravada Buddhism they helped to transmit to the Thais. Whereas Khmer stone sanctuaries only needed to be small to accommodate Hindu images and rituals involving a few high priests and royals, Thai chapels needed to be large to host assemblies of monks and the public. Thus, Thai builders used wood to construct larger roofs than could be built with stone. The size and mixed masonry-and-wood construction of temple halls are indirect legacies of the Mons, whose own structures survive mostly in the form of the barest ruins of chedis.

1.2 The Ayutthaya Period: 14th–18th centuries

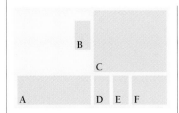

<table>
<tr><td></td><td>B</td><td></td></tr>
<tr><td></td><td>C</td><td></td></tr>
<tr><td>A</td><td>D E F</td><td></td></tr>
</table>

A. *Ayutthaya-era architecture is epitomised by its main palace,* Sanphet Prasat, *featuring a cruciform central hall with a spired roof, sweeping front and rear halls with multi-tiered telescoping roofs, and a bowed, raised base. It was destroyed in 1767.*

B. *Ayutthaya sculptors styled images of the Buddha wearing jewels and a crown, as the concept of kingship became intertwined with Buddhism.*

C. *The kingdom's royal temple was centred on the three brick* chedis *of Wat Phra Sri Sanphet, built in 1491.*

D. *The palace of Ayutthaya's Greek prime minister, Constantine Phaulkon, in Lopburi, is an early example of Western architecture in Siam.*

E. *Wat Ratburana's stately* prang *was erected in 1424 to enshrine a vast cache of relics. When unsealed in 1957, it held royal regalia, votive tablets and Buddha images, including antiquities from throughout Asia.*

F. *Phetchburi's Wat Ko Kaew Suttharam features the bowed base and windowless walls that are characteristic of the period.*

The 400-year period named after Siam's capital from 1351 to 1767 is the golden age of Thai architecture. Ayutthaya grew rich and powerful thanks to its military might, its exports of rice and its role as an entrepôt for Europe's trade with Japan and China. By the 17th century, Ayutthaya had become one of the world's great cities, with a population of one million and some 550 major buildings, including 400 temples. The capital was built some 60 km north of the present capital in Bangkok, on an island where the Chao Phraya River meets two other rivers.

Ayutthaya displaced the Khmer dominions in Siam, subdued Angkor in 1352, annexed Sukhothai and became an empire, often warring with Lanna and Burma. Khmer influence survived in Ayutthaya's language of administration and Siamese adoption of the concept of the divine king. During this period, architecture took on an imperial grandeur, the capital's temples and palaces glittering with golden spires.

Temple halls were built with thick walls, massive columns and narrow slits for windows. Both forms of the memorial tower—the *chedi* and *prang*—underwent stylistic evolution, becoming taller and thinner over the centuries. *Wats* typically featured a *prang* as the central element, another Khmer legacy.

Chinese cultural influence surged from the 13th through to the 15th centuries. Thais borrowed Chinese motifs from imported ceramics. They kilned ceramic roof tiles in Chinese shapes and adopted Chinese ornament such as lacquer painting and mother-of-pearl inlay.

From the mid-16th century, trade and diplomacy with Europe introduced Western forms to Thai architecture and ornament. Acanthus leaf designs were incorporated into *lai thai* motifs. Foreign influence peaked during the 17th-century reign of King Narai, when many high officials were of Japanese, Chinese, Indian and Persian origin; Prime Minister Constantine Phaulkon was Greek. French engineers built palaces and forts for the King in Ayutthaya, Lopburi and Bangkok. This cosmopolitanism set the stage for the further development of Siamese culture and architecture in the centuries that followed.

1.3 The Rattanakosin Period: 1782–present

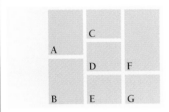

A. Outward looking: stained glass windows of Bangkok's Wat Benchamabophit, rebuilt in 1899 by King Rama V, are lucid examples of Siamese adaptation of Western ideas.

B. Lavish ornamentation conveys the Rattanakosin will to surpass Ayutthaya's lost architectural glories. Doors of the royal Wat Rachabophit are among the most elaborate portals in Thai architecture.

C. Thonburi's Wat Rachaworaviharn, with its Chinese-style roofs and crockery mosaic, typifies dozens of structures constructed or renovated between 1824 and 1851 by King Rama III, the Chakri dynasty's most prolific builder of temples.

D. A neoclassical-style palace. King Rama V built the Warophatphiman throne hall and royal residence in 1876 at Bang Pa-In summer palace near Ayutthaya. The Greek pediment and Corinthian columns are elements typical of the Classic Revival styles that proliferated in Europe from the mid-18th to the mid-19th centuries.

E. A Victorian-style throne hall: a one-storey timber structure with a central dome, Thewaratsaparom Throne Hall was built by King Rama V during the first decade of the 20th century in Bangkok's Phayathai Palace. It hosted ceremonies, theatrical performances and movie screenings.

F. King Rama IV, known as 'The Scholar-King', built Bangkok's marble-clad Wat Rachapradit in 1864 for the reformist Dhammayutika Buddhist sect that he founded. Murals inside depict the King, an accomplished astronomer, observing the 1868 eclipse of the sun, which he had accurately predicted.

G. Completed in 1933, Bangkok's Sala Chalerm Krung theatre was built in a modern style inspired by Europe's Bauhaus, by Prince Samaichalerm Krisdakorn. It hosts plays and screenings to this day.

The architecture for which Thailand is best known is represented by the spectacular palaces and temples built in Bangkok since the capital's founding in 1782. This period is called the Rattanakosin era, after the city's Thai name, which means 'jewelled city', referring to the Emerald Buddha enshrined at the Grand Palace. The Rattanakosin era, and the Chakri dynasty that established it, continue to today.

Rattanakosin's origins began with the Burmese destruction of Ayutthaya in 1767. Siam's capital was first moved by King Taksin to Thonburi, just across the river from Bangkok. The new kingdom lasted just 15 years. The Thonburi period, as it is called, saw little construction.

King Rama I, however, built ambitiously after founding Rattanakosin, in an effort to reconstruct not only infrastructure but national morale. He aimed to recapture the glory of Ayutthaya, and early Rattanakosin style followed Ayutthaya precedents closely. But from the mid-19th century onwards, Siamese architecture became increasingly dynamic, colourful and eclectic. Temple halls were built taller, lighter and more complex in structure and decoration. The murals inside them attained an unprecedented level of artistry, distinguishing the Rattanakosin period as the great era of Siamese painting.

Chinese stylistic influence resurged during the reign of King Rama III, thanks to extensive trade and diplomacy. The ceramic tiles covering palace and temple roofs began to be finished in coloured glazes. Crockery mosaic came into wide royal use, and some temple and palace roofs were done in Chinese style. Chinese stone statuary was imported to stand guard in temple and palace courtyards (see 8.1 Chinese Influence). Rama III was an especially prolific builder and renovator; most of the capital's *wats* and many structures in the Grand Palace show his influence.

Kings Rama IV, Rama V and Rama VI often built in Western style—both hybrid-style buildings like the Chakri Maha Prasat in the Grand Palace, and many royal and princely palaces in pure European styles (see 8.5 Western-Style Palaces and Mansions). The intent was political, to convey to the Western powers then colonising Asia that Siam stood as an equal. Given Siam's unique success in preserving its sovereignty, this architecture has a special historical significance as well as enduring aesthetic appeal.

Thai Houses

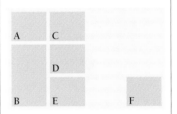

A. *A central-style wooden house at the Ancient City outdoor museum in Samut Prakan province.*

B. *When built along a waterway, the Siamese house is often fronted by a pavilion for relaxation, bathing and alighting from boats. This house stands at the Rose Garden Hotel in Nakhon Pathom.*

C. *Parallel twin cabins form one side of this cluster house, the former palace of the governor of Phattalung province, now a museum.*

D. *Northern houses feature low eaves and small window openings.*

E. *The traditional principle of construction from pre-assembled panels lends itself to low-cost houses improvised from corrugated metal, scrap wood and woven elements.*

F. *Waterways act as highways for houses along canals.*

Preceding pages: This Shan family in Muang Pon village in the northern province of Mae Hong Son stores grain in a rice barn adjacent to their main house.

Hinting at shared cultural origins, the primary form of dwelling throughout Southeast Asia and parts of East Asia is a gable-roofed structure built on posts. As depicted in ancient relics such as engraved bronze drums unearthed in Vietnam and Indonesia, this form dates to the region's prehistory. Thailand's version of the house is built of bamboo or unpainted wood, often near water, using pre-assembled walls that are hoisted into place on the posts, with a multi-purpose space below the cabin.

The most refined local expression of such architecture evolved in central Siam during the prosperous Ayutthaya period. A large house of this type may have three or more cabins grouped around a raised terrace that functions as an outdoor family room. This classic Siamese dwelling stands as one of Asia's most appealing types of traditional house, combining gracefulness with fluent adaptation to climate and lifestyle.

Similar structures evolved in Thailand's north, northeast and south. The northern version is somewhat more boxy and massive than its central cousin, with walls that slope out towards the roof rather than in, as they do in central-style construction. Northeastern houses are more rustic, while southern houses often feature Malay-influenced elements such as painted fretwork and hipped roofs descended from colonial architecture.

Most Thais still live off the land, mostly from paddy, the nation's leading farm export. Special architecture suiting the demands of rice cultivation include barns for storing grain and temporary shelters that farmers use when working in fields away from the village. These structures are so important that some farmers devote more attention to their construction and aesthetics than to their own houses. Like houses, these barns are usually built on posts, with gable roofs. A rice barn is typically part of the house compound, which has trees around the perimeter and other small sheds for storage or livestock. Plants are grown in pots or in patches in the garden for kitchen use or auspiciousness rather than decoration.

The merits of traditional houses have attracted growing numbers of affluent Thais and expatriates to invest years of effort and large sums of money in conserving them. Others build them from scratch at even greater expense, commissioning one of a few firms specialising in traditional construction.

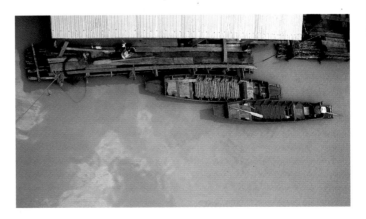

2.1 The Siamese Wooden House

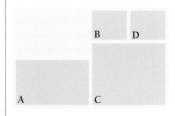

A. A basic cluster house with two living cabins and a sitting room called a ho nang, here built as an open pavilion. The slanting angles of posts, walls, windows and roofs lend stability.

B. Houses by rivers and canals are built facing the water, not the road. This new wooden house near Ko Kret island on the Chao Phraya River employs posts of concrete rather than timber, and an air-conditioned ho nang instead of an open pavilion.

C. A wealthy family may build a cluster of houses all at once, rather than adding cabins to a terrace over the years. These mansions, called ruen khahabodi, have flourishes like moulded wood panels and carved decoration on windows. This example in Nonthaburi accommodates homestays as The Thai House Hotel.

D. Thais traditionally place few plants directly around the house, affording clear access to the space underneath, which is used for family activities, storage or keeping livestock.

The classic wooden house of central Thailand is set apart by a certain elegance. It has a concave roof, arching bargeboards with hooked lower finials, and trapezoidal walls. These slopes and curving lines keep it from looking boxy.

The house's adaptation to heavy rain and heat starts with the tall posts on which the structure is built. This is needed because central Thai villages are mostly built near rivers and canals, which are subject to flooding during the wet season thats lasts from June to October. When the ground is dry, families use the sheltered area under the house, which is about 2 m to 2.5 m high, for making crafts, storing tools or raising chickens and ducks.

The curve of the steep roof is highlighted by a bowed plank called a bargeboard, or *panlom*, placed at the gable rims to protect the roof tiles or thatch from wind. The lower ends of the bargeboards are carved in a horn-like shape called a *ngao*.

Columns and walls are built leaning inwards, adding structural strength. Windows are tall and wide, for optimum ventilation; their shape mirrors the trapezoid of the cabin wall panels. Skilled carpenters pre-assemble the wall panels in a standardised, modular system that allows them to be used interchangeably in any Thai house. The rooms open onto covered verandahs about 2 m wide, which step down onto a broad wooden terrace.

A family might start with a single cabin and terrace, using a small cabin to the side as a kitchen. As the family grows, they will add two cabins at a time to reach a total of three or five; an even number of living cabins is considered inauspicious.

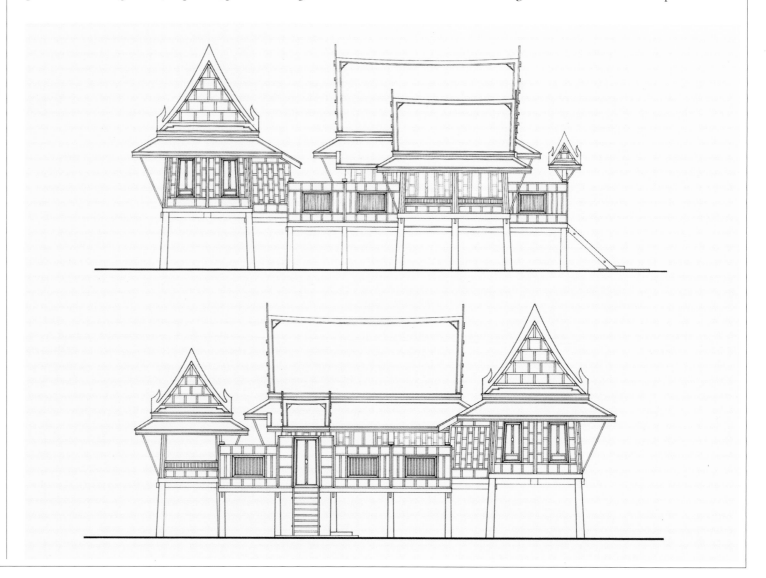

A. *A missing bargeboard plank exposes the thatched roof of this house to the elements.*

B. *The Siamese wooden house at its simplest: a single cabin and verandah. A central terrace and more cabins can be added as a family grows.*

C. *Gold leaf and ornately carved elements such as eave brackets mark this stately cluster house as a royal abode. Formerly a royal residence of King Rama I, today it serves as a scripture pavilion, or ho trai, at Thonburi's Wat Rakhang.*

2.2 The Northern House

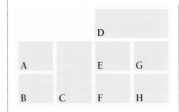

The architecture of local houses symbolises the distinctive culture of northern Thailand, a region known as Lanna, the name of the kingdom centred there from the 13ᵗʰ to the 18ᵗʰ centuries. The largest and most refined type of Lanna residence is the classic timber *kalae* house, named for the V- or X-shaped wooden decoration extending from the gable end peaks, thought to represent the horns of the water buffalo.

The *kalae* house, like its central Siamese cousin, is assembled from pre-carpentered wooden panels, on a platform over wooden stilts, with a multi-purpose space below the cabin. The house typically has twin cabins joined at the eaves along a rain gutter, with wooden tiles on the roof rather than ceramic. Walls on the lateral sides lean quite steeply outward towards the roof, not inward as in the central house. The roof is not as steep and curved as the central version, so the slopes form a triangular pediment. Windows are small and placed only on the lateral walls, the better to retain heat during the cool season, when temperatures sometimes drop close to freezing.

There are four different types of the *kalae* house, which vary in size and floor plan to include as many as four cabins as well as secondary terraces. Other types of northern houses are smaller and less luxurious than the *kalae* but share many of its basic features.

The northern house's most important part is the terrace and *toen*, or verandah, usually built facing south for warmth, a centre for family activities, entertaining guests and sometimes sleeping. The main cabin has a single room that serves as a bedroom for the whole family.

2.3 The Northeastern House

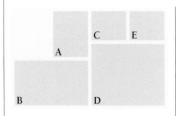

A. A northeastern house begins with the construction of a single large cabin. A second cabin is added when a daughter marries, a tradition that keeps the son-in-law close to help with farming, and prevents conflicts between his wife and his mother. Sons move out upon marriage.

B. Walls of the northeastern house are built of planks, not pre-assembled panels as in the central region. This house is at the Museum of Isaan Houses, Mahasarakham province.

C. An Isaan adage says that one of the seven joys of life as a human is owning a large house with a wood-shingled roof. This duplex is located in Khorat province.

D. The second roof eave on the right side of this house covers a deep verandah built on a lower level than the cabin. Beyond the verandah is the terrace on a still lower level, seen at far right.

E. A northeastern house in Mukdahan province, at Wat Song Khon, a Catholic church.

Centuries of migration from nearby Laos have helped shape the architecture of Thailand's northeast, known as Isaan. Siam gained control of the region in the 18th century, and from the early 19th century promoted the resettlement of Lao immigrants there. Today the Tai Lao peoples outnumber the Khmer and other ethnic minorities in Isaan's 19 provinces, where a third of Thailand's population lives.

The region's culture is rich, but shaped by chronic economic hardships resulting from a dry climate, poor soil and a less developed education infrastructure in rural areas. Its architecture, in turn, is simpler and less decorated than elsewhere in Thailand.

Northeastern-style houses are similar to central Thai houses. They are built of wood on stilts, but their roofs feature a gentler slope since there is less rain to cope with. Thatch and corrugated iron roofs are more common in Isaan than other regions. Walls are perpendicular, not slanted, and often made of simple wooden planks rather than the prefabricated panels used in other regions.

Homes are built in a compound structure, starting with a main cabin; a second cabin may be added as the family grows.

2.4 The Southern House

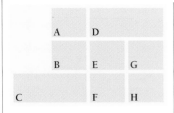

A. Fretted wood ornament is a Malay-influenced characteristic of southern architecture, as seen on this hipped-gable roof.

B. This Thai Muslim house in Pattani province has two entrances and staircases, one for males and one for females, as per religious precept.

C. A blend of central and southern style: carved and fretted wood in geometric and floral designs decorate the 19th-century monks' houses at Wat Wang Tawantok in Nakhon Sri Thammarat.

D. Front and side elevations of a Thai Muslim house in typical duplex format, with a hipped-gable or blanor roof. The verandah and its staircase are reserved for male members of the family, while the cabin at the rear houses a kitchen and second staircase for females (not shown). The house is built on multiple levels, with living cabins on the highest platform.

E. As per southern practice, no fence is built around the yard of this Muslim house on Samui island. Posts are concrete, or concrete-encased wood, for durability in a wet climate.

F. A monk's house designed to stay dry in southern rain, with a hipped roof of terra cotta tiles, a broad eave over the verandah and a second eave projecting over the stairs, located at Wat Manmaung Moo in Songkhla.

G. A 1905 photo, taken during King Rama V's visit, shows houses in the palace compound of the Sultan of Terangganu—then affiliated with Siam, but now a Malaysian state. The pyramidal roofs typify Malay and Javanese architecture. Woven wall panels show the geometric patterns of Malay craft.

H. A hipped roof, known as a lima or panya roof, tops this Thai Muslim house in Surat Thani province. The verandah is hung with bird cages, probably for the melodious Java doves popular with southern men.

Of several styles of houses in the 14 provinces of Thailand's south, the most characteristic is the Thai Muslim house with its distinctly Malay features. These houses are especially common in the four deep south provinces of Pattani, Satun, Yala and Narathiwat, where most of the populace are Muslims of Malay ethnicity.

The roofs of these houses take one of three forms. Hipped roofs, known as *panya* or *lima*, are popular, an influence from colonial Dutch or English architecture that spread from Indonesia or the Malay peninsula. The same is true of the hipped-gable roof, which is called a *blanor* roof locally. Gable roofs are also common.

Malay style, with its roots in Islamic art, is expressed in carved ornamental details: gable end panels, roof finials and the fretwork of ventilation grilles, often painted in many colours.

The posts of southern houses of all sorts typically stand on column bases, or *teen sao*, made of stone or cement placed on the ground rather than sunk into it. This protects the posts against termites and moisture during the rainy season. This feature also allows the building to be relocated.

2.5 Houses on Water

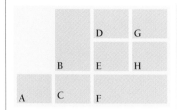

A. A floating house busy with trade, in early Rattanakosin times.

B. A raft house in Uthai Thani. Note the hinged wall propped up to open the cabin room to the water.

C. More raft houses and waterfront post houses in Uthai Thani province, in the heart of the central region.

D. The posts of houses by the water need to be high enough to accommodate seasonal flooding.

E. The walkway of this house probably leads to a pavilion along the main waterway.

F. Lost Bangkok: thatched roofs once formed the city's skyline.

G. Semi-traditional houses, like these in Ayutthaya, epitomise the style popular in central Thailand since the mid-20th century. The steep concave roof of the house on the left gives a more traditional appearance to its cabin, which is built simply of wooden planks rather than trapezoidal panels. The roof of the cabin on the right has a straight, low slope. The use of metal allows for a simpler profile than the traditional roof, which is shaped to prevent leaks through the thatch or tiles.

H. Waterways of the central region are dotted with Muslim communities, marked by handsome homes like this one.

From the vantage point of the traditional Thai lifestyle, with its heavy reliance on boat travel, fishing and frequent bathing, the only place better to live than next to a river is right on top of one, in a house on stilts or pontoons. These homes are comfortable and well suited to commerce, given the ease of water transport.

A raft house, or *ruen pae*, can be built much like a house on land, with a gable roof, low eaves and wood- or bamboo-panelled walls. The cabin wall facing the water, usually made of woven bamboo or corrugated iron, has hinges so it can be propped open, often to display goods for sale to passing boats. The house can be built with single, twin or even three cabins, each about 4 m by 6 m. Rooms are used flexibly for sleeping, cooking, handicraft production, storage and trade. Bathing is done directly in the surrounding water, so no bathroom is needed. Below the cabin is the pontoon, made of wood or bundles of bamboo, which rises or falls with the tide and floats over floods. This feature also allows the house to be relocated.

The tall posts that prop up the traditional Thai house allow it to be built directly over a canal, river or lake with little redesign. It is then called a *baan rim naam*, meaning 'house by the water'. Sometimes, part of the house is built over land, but it can easily be built entirely on water with a walkway leading to shore. In either case, the main entrance will face the water, usually with a covered verandah and stairs leading down into the water, for ease of bathing and transfer from boats.

2.6 Bamboo Houses

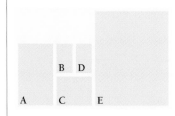

A. *A nicely crafted verandah balustrade fronts this petite house on display at Chiang Mai University. The roof is thatched with tong tung (dipterocarp) leaves often used in northern construction.*

B. *Bamboo is often combined with load-bearing elements made of wood.*

C. *A hill tribe house in Mae Jan village, Chiang Rai.*

D. *Walls woven as neatly as a basket.*

E. *The art of woven architecture is especially distinctive among ethnic Malay communities in the south, as seen in this photo from Terangganu, a sultanate loosely affiliated with Siam when the picture was taken in 1905. The photographer probably accompanied King Rama V during his visit there. In 1909, the King ceded the territory to Britain, and today it is a state in Malaysia.*

The structural characteristics of Thai bamboo houses are much the same as wooden ones: one-storey, raised on stilts, a gable roof and prefabricated walls. They tend to be smaller, however, with a single cabin, not clusters grouped around a big terrace as in the case of some wooden houses.

Dwellings of bamboo can be considered the primary form of the traditional Thai house—the type in which most commoners used to live and the original basis for forms later deployed in the wooden version. The Thai system of pre-assembled wall panels, for example, probably evolved from bamboo houses since wall mats needed to be woven as a complete unit before being erected, a technique that proves efficient when building with wood.

Bamboo houses are still built among low-income families and also for temporary use; for example, as a 'starter' house for newlyweds waiting to build a wooden house. Bamboo structures can be built by householders themselves without using hired craftsmen.

A house can be made almost entirely from bamboo, but other materials are commonly used as well. Posts and beams, for example, may be of wood for greater strength, relegating bamboo to roofs, joists and floors. Walls are woven of split bamboo, palm leaves or, in the south, pandan leaves.

In central Thai parlance, the structure is called *ruen khrueng phook* (house assembled by binding), while in the north, it is known as *ruen mai bua*. Low income levels in many districts in the northeast keep the bamboo house in favour there because it is inexpensive.

In the south, bamboo houses are most common among fishing communities. Those in Muslim districts are remarkable for the beautiful geometric woven patterns of their walls: herringbone, diamonds, stars and others.

2.7 Rice Barns

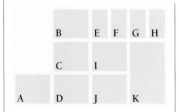

	B		E	F	G	H
			C		I	
A			D		J		K

A. An A-frame rice barn in Mae Hong Son.

B. A rice barn typical of the style seen in Chiang Mai's Mae Rim district. An eave is extended at the building's side to create a shed for tool storage.

C. A rice barn in the northeastern province of Roi Et. The eaves extend far beyond the walls to keep the grain dry.

D. A rice barn typical of those built in the central and northeastern regions.

E. A typical northern granary with a balcony that projects beyond the posts on all four sides.

F & G. Rice barns in the northeast.

H. A rice barn at the Chiang Rai house of painter Thawan Duchanee (see 9.6 An Artist's Desmesne: The Thawan Duchanee House).

I. Ventilation grilles in walls help to keep rice dry when in storage.

J. A neat and sturdy northeastern rice barn.

K. An assortment of rice barns in various styles.

Rural homes each have a rice barn or granary (*yung khao*), built to protect the product from spoilage and vermin. The granary is virtually the family's cash box, since rice is farmed mostly as a cash crop and needs to be stored for sale. A large rice barn marks a farm as prosperous. A family that lacks a granary and simply stores rice in the house is probably farming the grain only for sustenance.

In most of Thailand, the granary is a rectangular cabin built on stilts, parallel to the main house but far enough away to maximise sunlight and ventilation so that the grain keeps dry. Gable roofs are common, and are usually made from corrugated iron or earthenware tiles nowadays instead of traditional thatch. Sometimes the underside is built with wooden walls to form an enclosed space for storing tools.

In the north, the barn is called *long khao*, *yung khao* or *ye khao*. It has massive pillars and a balcony on all four sides, making the cabin appear to float in mid-air. The roof may be either gabled or in the hipped form called *panya*. Northeastern granaries usually resemble local houses, with metal gable roofs and small entrance terraces suitable for keeping tools.

In the south, soil conditions are less suitable for rice farming, and paddy is usually grown in small quantities for family use, not trade. For this reason, the southern house is likely to have a simple rice room inside instead of a separate barn. When a full granary is built, called a *ruen khao* locally, it is usually smaller than its counterparts in other regions.

2.8 Field Huts and Cottages

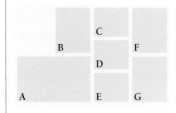

A. Huts and cottages in the northern province of Mae Hong Son.

B. A simple hut in a rice field in Phitsanulok province. The front eave projects over a low platform, while a gable roof covers a higher platform—useful when it rains.

C. A cottage in Mae Hong Son, simple but adequate for stays of several months a year while tending to upland fields. Structural elements are made of wood, and simple balustrades serve as walls.

D. A field cottage in Sukhothai province.

E. A field hut in Mae Hong Son. This roof profile, formed by the deep eave on the right, is called tup nok kwaek, after its resemblance to a bird.

F. Another Mae Hong Son field cottage, combining a metal gable roof with a thatched eave.

G. A bamboo-walled field hut in Phichit province, equipped with its own artesian well.

When farmers live several kilometres from their rice fields, they need to build huts and cottages (*haang na*) for shelter while working. Most sheds are simple, temporary shelters for daily rest or short visits. In hilly areas, however, rice fields are scattered further away from the community, and cottages need to be built for longer, more comfortable stays of four to six months.

Such field cottages are found throughout the northern provinces, where they are known *theng na*. These cottages are a bit like primary homes in the village, but are more quaint and charming.

Rice farming has surged in some northeastern provinces since irrigation works were built there in recent decades. Field huts or *thiang na* have became numerous, but are constructed simply, in a folkish style. The gable roof is easily assembled, and the house is only slightly elevated, since flooding is infrequent in the region. In the central region, field cottages are less common because rice fields are located close to the village. In the south, cottages are few because rice is not farmed much compared to other crops, such as rubber, that have different work patterns and requirements.

2.9 Roadside Shops, Stalls and Pavilions

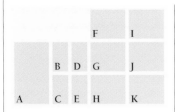

A. *Simple pavilions descended from field huts have become fixtures of Thailand's architecture for leisure and travel, like this restaurant booth overlooking the Gulf of Siam in Rayong province. Furniture for outdoor use is often made of painted cement.*

B. *Reclaimed wood from old farm tools and carts is used to create pavilions that combine architecture and furniture in a single structure. These are often used in restaurants and resorts. This one sports northern-style kalae finials and fretwork.*

C. *A bus-stop pavilion with traditional roof details, balustrades and other features derived from central-style houses.*

D. *A roadside shelter built around its own shade tree.*

E. *Roadside vendors still build their own stalls, but kiosks can now be bought ready-made. Bamboo construction is inexpensive, light enough to transport by hand, and helps to brand one's product as authentic.*

F. *Farmers turn highways into drive-through shopping malls. These women in Chanthaburi tempt motorists with fried chips made from the province's famous fruit, the durian.*

G, H & J. *The architectural features of the Thai shop take a back seat to the profusion of goods spilling out onto the street.*

I. *Unlike ethnic Chinese merchants, Thais used to build their shophouses on one storey. A few survive far from the beaten path, like this one in Nan province.*

K. *Building a kiosk takes little but a roof and perhaps a second eave that can be unfolded against the rain or late afternoon sunshine. Vendors focus on perfecting their products, like the sweet roti crêpes made by these Ayutthaya women.*

Until Bangkok's canals started to be filled in and covered with roads in the 1950s, transport was mostly by water and selling was done directly from boats. Boats were also used to bring goods to traders, who set up riverside stalls and shophouses. When transport shifted to land, rows of shops sprouted along roads instead of the waterways. Today, roads throughout Thailand, even deep in the countryside, are lined with wooden stalls and shophouses selling local produce, handmade items and packaged goods.

The simplest type is a small lean-to or shed (*ran kha rim thang*) standing by the road at the edge of a field. It may feature a bamboo table with seats attached, and a roof of palm thatch. Other stalls are built for temporary use, such as when fruit or vegetables are in season. At intersections in town, groups of stalls often spring up together and eventually become a continuous row of permanent shops.

More elaborate is the traditional Thai shophouse or *ran ruen*, used for both trade and living. It is a wooden house built with a front verandah where goods are displayed. The verandah is sheltered from the sun and rain by an extended roof eave. Unlike its Chinese-style counterparts (see 8.2 Chinese Shophouses), the Thai shophouse is built on a single storey, with space for the family to live in the main room behind the sales verandah, not upstairs on a second or third floor. It is against Thai custom to stand higher than a person's head, a part of the body considered sacred, so traditional buildings are constructed on one storey.

Other huts and pavilions include roadside shelters for bus passengers and booths for outdoor restaurants.

House Elements

The beauty of the traditional Thai house is achieved with almost no decoration. Its aesthetics are embodied in its form and structure: the shapes of the elements, and the lines and proportions of the building as a whole. Its colours and surface textures are raw and natural—unpainted wood and unglazed clay roof tiles. Pure ornament is limited to the carved wooden panels, or *yong*, that decorate the exterior base of the windows in well-appointed houses, and the geometric grid of classic wall panels. Also decorative are roof elements such as the wooden horns called *kalae*, used in the north. Otherwise, ornament is reserved for palace and temple architecture.

Despite the curves and trapezoidal shape of the structure, neatness is achieved because the house is essentially built from a kit. A master carpenter and his assistants construct most of the house elements, including the wall panels, windows and roof structure, before the project is erected. Since joinery is used rather than nails, each piece has to be fashioned with great care to ensure it fits.

The important parts of the house are on the outside. Waking hours are spent engaged in family activities on the verandah and terrace, below the house or in the yard. Interiors are dimly illuminated and minimally furnished.

Because good wood is now scarce and carpentry expensive, building a traditional house today is often a matter of recycling components from disused structures. This is fitting because tradition intended the components to be used as interchangeable modules for deployment in any house. Elements made of teak, in particular, can last more than 200 years; a few houses still in use have posts and walls dating to the 18th century.

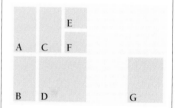

A. The broad leaves of the *tung* tree thatch the roof of this rice barn.

B. The exterior of a rice barn, built with studs on the outside, forming a smooth surface on the inside.

C. Thatched roofs and woven walls are primordial elements of the Southeast Asian house, as in this example in Phayao province.

D. The verandah of a Shan house in Muang Pon, Mae Hong Son.

E. Roof shingles made from reclaimed wood at the Anantara Resort and Spa in Chiang Rai.

F. A fretted wooden panel decorates the window of a Siamese house on Ko Phra island in Ayutthaya.

G. Traditional construction relies solely on joinery.

Preceding pages: The classic Siamese house wears its architecture on the surface. Made entirely of wood, except when thatch or ceramic roof coverings are used, the house elements function superbly to protect the structure against weather. This house can be found in King Rama II Memorial Park in Samut Songkhram province.

3.1 Gable Roofs

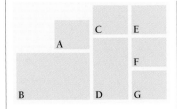

A. *The horizontality of the Siamese cluster house gets a strong sense of lift from the rising lines of the gable roof ends. This mansion stands in Rama II Memorial Park, Samut Songkhram province.*

B. *Kansaad eaves project beyond the main roof to shield walls. Rain gutters are a modern feature of this house in Hua Hin.*

C. *Unglazed earthenware tiles have been the most popular house roof covering since the mid-20ᵗʰ century. Earlier, thatch or wood shingles were prevalent.*

D. *Kansaad eaves over this entrance are supported by posts and brackets.*

E. *The central Siamese roof is steep and concave to sluice rain off quickly so that the covering does not leak or rot.*

F. *Traditional and semi-traditional gable roofs in Ayutthaya. The cabins on the right have been added to an older, traditional-style house with a tall, concave roof. Steep roofs have gone out of style now that modern roof coverings cut costs by allowing a simpler, flatter structure.*

G. *Roofs of this southern house have steep, straight slopes.*

The gable roof is Thailand's traditional roof form. It is built with a steep concave shape in the central region, where total rainfall during the wettest month, September, exceeds 30 cm, most of which comes in a daily torrent lasting an hour or less. The roof's concave shape copes with this intensity well, sluicing water down and shooting it out past the walls to prevent it from seeping through the roof covering.

Additional rain and sun protection is provided by a short eave below the main roof on two or all four sides extending about 40 cm from the wall. One or more sides of the house may also, or instead, feature longer *kansaad* eaves supported by brackets. Typical roof coverings are terra cotta tiles, teak shingles, corrugated iron or palm leaf thatch.

The height of the roof helps not only with rain but with keeping the inside cool. The interior has no ceiling, so the large space of the roof cavity allows hot air to rise up and away from the living space, then escape through openings under the eaves.

Regional variations are adapted to climate and culture. Cooler weather in the north calls for the roof to dip lower to window level, and its plane is not concave. Roofs of homes in the south are large and steep to cope with heavy rains and winds. The aridity of the northeast allows for roofs of relatively gentle slope.

3.2 Hipped and Hipped-Gable Roofs

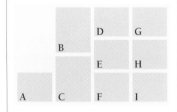

A. This Shan house in Mae Hong Son province features an extended eave below its hipped-gable roof.

B. The hipped-gable roof form adds a small gable to a hipped roof configuration to provide better ventilation of heat.

C. Hipped-gable or blanor roofs common in the south often feature wooden or stucco finials.

D. Hipped-roofed raft houses on the Sakaekrang river in Uthai Thani province. In the background is the octagonal mondop of Wat Uposatharam.

E. A hipped-gable roof of corrugated metal in Ayutthaya province.

F. A house with a hipped roof in Thonburi, probably dating to the late 19th or early 20th century.

G. A hipped-gable roof with deep secondary eaves on a house in Nan.

H. A house in Mae Hong Son province with a hipped-gable roof.

I. Another Nan house with a hipped-gable roof.

Although gable roofs are prevalent, hipped and hipped-gable roofs have long been used in Thailand, reflecting Malay, colonial and Western influences.

The hipped roof, sloping on all four sides for better drainage, is called *panya* in Thailand. It is found on some Thai Muslim houses in the south, where it is called a *lima* roof, a Malay term derived from the Arabic word for five, referring to the roof's five ridges. This roof form is believed to have been introduced by British and Dutch colonials in the Malay archipelago from the 17th century onwards. Hipped roofs also appear on some houses and other buildings built by Straits Chinese immigrants in the Sino-Portuguese style.

Hipped roofs were used on many royal residences, government buildings and mansions built during the reigns of kings Rama IV, Rama V and Rama VI in a variety of European styles (see 8.5 Western-Style Palaces and Mansions). Here, the form was a direct Western influence, not a style brought from the south. This legacy has helped to popularise the hipped roof form throughout Thailand over the past 100 years.

The hipped-gable, gambrel or Manila roof, common on Thai Muslim homes in the south, combines the hipped form with gables midway up the slope on two or more sides. This adds better ventilation to the drainage advantages of the hipped roof. It is known in Thailand as a *blanor* roof, from an Indonesian word referring to the Dutch, and reflecting the colonial origins of the style. As with the hipped roof, this form appeared atop many Bangkok palaces and mansions built during the late 19th and early 20th centuries, and its use has spread widely since that time.

3.3 Roof Finials

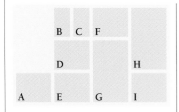

A. Lower bargeboard finials of two adjoining gable roofs on a house in Chiang Mai province, in a simple kranok motif.

B. A fish tail-style finial on a riverside house in Ayutthaya province.

C. The horn-like tua ngao bargeboard finial is the central region's predominant type, believed by some to have been derived from the head or tail of the mythical naga.

D. A contemporary tua ngao finial with carved decoration.

E. Another northern-style bargeboard finial with carved kranok motif.

F. Fretted wooden roof finials decorate the gables of Thai Muslim houses and others.

G. A southern-style finial on a house in Pattani province.

H. Apex finials in a style used in Mae Cham, a Thai Lue district in Chiang Mai. The finials are perforated to let the wind flow through.

I. The X-shaped kalae finials of this northern Thai house are an attached decoration rather than an extension of the bargeboards, with carved kranok motifs.

The main decorative feature of the central Siamese house roof is the bargeboard, or *panlom*, the long, thin plank that covers the edge of the roof at the gable ends. It has a practical function, which is to keep wind from displacing the roof tiles or thatch, but it also has pleasing aesthetics: a graceful curve rising to a narrow peak, which accentuates the roof's height, steepness and shape.

In a timber house, the *panlom* is made of a wooden board about 3 cm thick. It is cut at an acute angle on the top end, where it joins its mate at the gable's peak. At its lower end, the bargeboard may be carved into a curved figure called a *tua ngao*. The commonest figure is that of a *ngao*, a stylised *naga* head that looks like a hook or fin pointing up towards the top of the gable. Carpenters may instead carve this decoration in the figure of a fish tail, called a *hang pla*, used mostly in the central and southern regions.

In northern Thailand, the finest houses are distinguished by the crossed boards placed at the peak of the *panlom*, called a *kalae*. This can be formed simply by extension of the *panlom* boards, or by attaching separate pieces of wood. The *kalae's* origin and meaning have been much debated. Some observers believe it resembles the horns of the water buffalo, a symbol indicating that the household can afford plenty of livestock (or would like to).

Houses in the south often have roof bargeboards with decorative wooden fretwork below the gable eaves as well as gable-peak finials of metal, stucco, or turned or fretted wood. In northeastearn houses, the *panlom* is usually a simple board with no lower finial.

3.4 Pediments

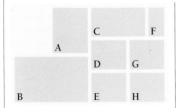

A. A pediment detached from a roof and displayed for sale at a roadside shop in Ayutthaya.

B. A classic central-style pediment incorporating luk fak-style wall panels.

C. Wooden pediment variations. Top row: variations of the phra athit or sunray design. Bottom row, from left: luk fak-wall panel style; horizontal planks; and the kan tan or palmyra palm leaf style.

D. Horizontally placed planks form a simple style of pediment.

E. A pediment with a ventilation grille on a house in Songkhla province.

F. Thatch ventilates hot air and blocks the rain.

G. A pediment using woven palm leaf in Songkhla province.

H. A ventilated pediment in the phra athit design above a kitchen.

The pediments of common houses are called *na chua*. They enclose the gable ends of the roof to protect the interior from the sun, wind and rain. Usually made of wood, *na chua* can be built in any one of several styles common to the central region and elsewhere.

Most popular is the rectangular frame pattern called *chua luk fak pakon*, which is also used for the wall panel style called *fa pakon*. On the pediment, the panels create a kind of pyramid design: a row of rectangles at the base narrow to just one at the top. A pediment design often used in the kitchen cabin is the *chua bai prue*, which is made of horizontal slats with openings for ventilation. Similarly, the popular *chua phra athit* motif, a sunray design, can be assembled with gaps for ventilation when used over a kitchen.

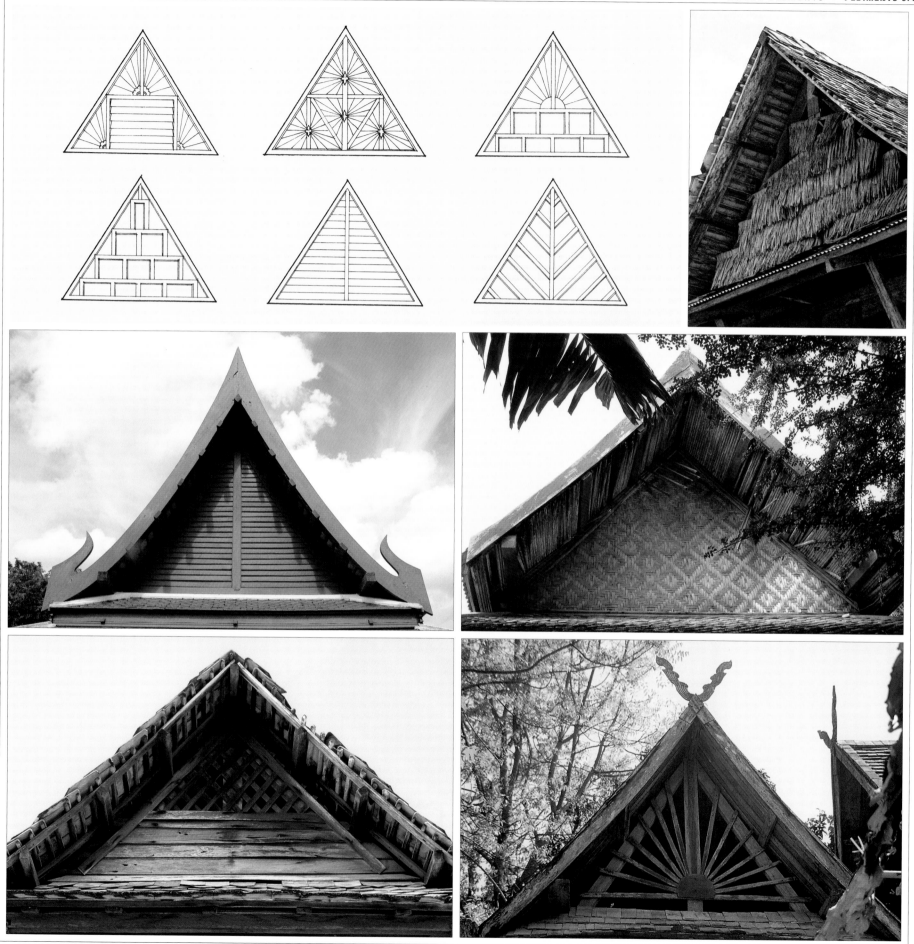

3.5 Walls

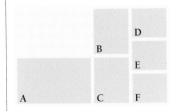

A. Walls of this contemporary house are decorated with wood panels styled after the tall rectangular grid pattern of traditional fa pakon wall modules.

B. Four of the many types of traditional wall panels (clockwise from top left): fa samruad *feature vertical bamboo or timber poles each standing a palm's width apart, connected by horizontal poles and laced with woven material, leaves or thatch, often used in kitchen cabins;* fa khad tae *have vertical poles of timber or bamboo, with woven split rattan or split bamboo in between, also useful in kitchens; the fanciest type of* fa kradan *panel, with moulded elements, called* fa lukfak kradan dun; *and a wall panel in the typical* fa pakon *style.*

C. Wall panels of pandanus grass woven in a handsome herringbone pattern with a wood frame in the southern province of Songkhla.

D. Classic fa pakon wall panels clad this cabin. Note the broader rectangles of the horizontal panels below the windows.

E. Wall with openings for ventilation that can be closed using a sliding panel. This feature is often found in houses in the north, like this one in Mae Hong Son.

F. Wall panels in the fa kradan reab style, which simply use planks fastened horizontally, common in the north and northeast. This house stands in Lampang.

One of the ingenuities of the Thai house is its fast and sturdy construction using modular wooden wall panels. Pre-assembled by carpenters, they are brought to the house site and simply hoisted into place on the posts, allowing a house to be erected in a single day. Wooden *fa* wall panel forms are named according to the pattern formed by the boards: *fa pakon* is the characteristic pattern of central Thai wall panels, a grid of tall rectangles.

The panels can be taken down almost as quickly to allow the house to be moved and reassembled elsewhere. Or they can be reused to build another house, thanks to their standard format. Panels are traditionally attached to the posts and beams using joinery rather than nails, which makes for a sturdier structure because it is not weakened when the wood expands or contracts in response to moisture or changes in temperature.

The modules are made in different shapes for different parts of the house. In a central Siamese house, with walls and posts that slope in towards the roof, panels on the narrow ends of the house are shaped like a tall trapezoid with a wide base and narrow top. The panels and uprights of northern houses taper in the opposite direction. Walls stand straight in the northeast, where builders favour rectangular-shaped walls; square is considered inauspicious. Northeastern house walls are also generally not pre-assembled, but simply nailed onto the posts horizontally in a pattern called *fa kradan reab* (panel of flat/smooth planks).

Bamboo houses use pre-woven wall panels; a practice which is likely the origin of pre-assembly in wooden houses. The interior walls of bamboo houses, and often wooden houses too, are made of woven panels called *fa samruad*, laced into a grid pattern.

fa samruad

fa khad tae

fa pakon

fa lukfak kradan dun

3.6 Doors

A. Fretted wood ventilation grille in a Chinese-influenced swastika design.

B. Carved wood ventilation grille over a door in the southern province of Pattani.

C. A simple latch with a single bolt.

D. Single-bolt wooden door latch on the inside of a door panel.

E. Door handle in a traditional diamond shape.

F. A modern lock design based on the diamond-shape form of a traditional door handle.

G & H. Latches of wood and metal.

I–O. A variety of doors. Terrace doors are wider.

Doors (*pratoo*) are usually just plain wooden panels, although wealthy residences may sport carved, painted or even gilded panels and frames. In a central Siamese house, the door's trapezoidal shape enhances the visual composition of the whole structure because it mirrors the wall and window shapes, narrowing from base to top. Each house cabin has a single door, which features two tall panels.

For good luck, house doors should be the width of three lengths of the owner's foot, or four lengths for the gable-topped gate at the terrace entrance above the main stairs. Northern Thais believe a guardian spirit resides within the frame of the door, so they avoid stepping on the threshold, which is painted red for auspiciousness.

A central-style house door has four main components: frame, panels, mullion and twin bolt. The frame is called a *thoranee*, formed by the horizontal parts. These correspond to a lintel and doorsill—wooden boards at the top and bottom that hold the dowels on which the vertical door panels swing. The *thoranee* frame of a door is mounted on a high threshold to block the entry of animals and water, and must be deliberately stepped over when coming or going. The panels of wood that open and close are called *baan*, and are usually made from teak to withstand hot, humid weather and the attack of termites.

One of the *baan* panels has a mullion, or *ok lao*, a narrow lip of wood fixed on the outside vertical edge to cover the gap when closed. Midway up the *ok lao* is a handle formed by a diamond-shaped block of wood, which, in refined homes, may have carved or painted designs. A wooden twin bolt called a *dan khuu* is mounted on the inside.

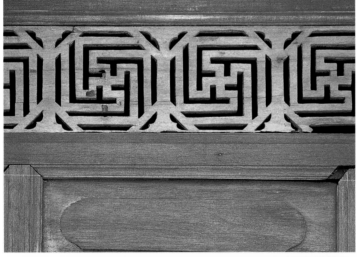

3.7 Windows

A–C. The carved wooden panel called yong decorates the exterior base of windows in central-style construction.

D. A wooden peg called a kob is fastened into a slot to lock the window panels shut from the interior.

E. A sliding panel opens this window grille for ventilation or light.

F–P. An assortment of window forms. The classic central style is seen in photo N, with dual leafs and a slight taper from base to top, set within a fa pakon wall module.

Windows (*naatang*) in central-style architecture are similar to doors in structure and mechanism. One window is built into each standard-size section of wall panel between the columns, except along the verandah, where one or two doors are installed. (A count of nine windows and doors is considered inauspicious because it corresponds to the nine openings of the human body.)

The window usually has a single-bolt lock, or *darn diao*, and a wooden bolt at the base called a *kob* that slots into the sill. At the base of the window on the outside, there is usually a fixed panel of carved wood called a *yong*. Though often purely ornamental, *yong* are sometimes fretted to provide ventilation.

Regional houses in the north, northeast and south often have other window types, such as single-panel or balustraded windows that close using a hinged or sliding board on the inside. Windows in the north and northeast tend to be smaller, with fewer per room.

3.8 Interiors

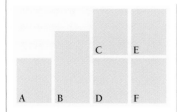

A. *Aristocratic furnishings in old Rattanakosin style decorate the Bangkok home of architect Lek Bunnag.*

B. *A traditional kitchen with a clay-lined platform that serves as a hearth. Gaps in the floor planks allow for fast drainage of water.*

C. *A home Buddha altar more elaborate than in some temples, at Suan Pakkad, a Bangkok palace built in traditional Thai style.*

D. *A bedroom at Kamthieng House. The cloth strung across the room is a mosquito net.*

E. *A cabin interior at the northern-style Kamthieng House, the 19th-century house of a rice farmer that has become a museum at Bangkok's Siam Society.*

F. *A colonial-style Bangkok house formerly owned by Jim Thompson Silk designer Gerald Pearce. Sparsely furnished, the atmosphere is open and airy for tropical living.*

The virtue of a traditional timber house interior is simplicity: the beauty of unpainted wood, and the versatility of open, uncluttered space. Rooms are little used except for slumber, so loose furniture is limited to cupboards and boxes for storage, and perhaps a small low table and cushions.

There are no ceiling panels, which reduces weight on the posts and exposes the underside of the roof for easier repairs. The space under the roof can be used for storage by placing crossed bamboo poles between the pillars.

The cabin may be partitioned into rooms by wooden or woven walls. But the floor plan remains simple, either a single room or one room bisected, not structured with hallways. In a cabin with two rooms, the larger one might be used as a sleeping area, while the smaller one houses an altar with a Buddha image. The family's unmarried daughters always take the innermost room.

Bedding is aligned parallel to the narrow end of the cabin rather than along the length, which is associated with the alignment of a body in a coffin. The alignment must also allow occupants to sleep with their heads pointing north, south or east, not west. This direction is associated with death; a corpse is displayed with its head facing west before cremation.

One cabin, or part of one, may be turned into a three-walled sitting room open on the verandah side. The kitchen or *ho khrua*, is situated on the terrace in a separate cabin somewhat behind the main house, and is just two posts wide. It features ventilation grilles in the pediments, walls and floors. Traditionally, the house had no bathroom. Bathing was done right on the terrace using a vat of water and a ladle. Toilet facilities were a chamberpot or nearby field or canal.

3.9 Terraces

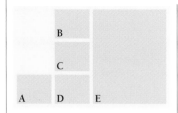

A. A northern-style terrace at a kalae house in Phrae province that now serves as a restaurant.

B. The broad terrace is the focal point of a Siamese cluster house.

C. The terrace of an aristocratic Siamese house often centres on an open pavilion, or ho klang, as seen at the Khun Phaen House in Ayutthaya province.

D. The terrace provides a semi-enclosed outdoor space that is bright, neat and dry, well suited to family activities, ceremonies such as weddings, and keeping a pot garden. This terrace is at the Thai compound built at the Nakhon Pathom campus of Mahidol University.

E. A deeply delightful terrace feature is the shade tree growing up through a well in the centre, epitomised at the splendid Thonburi mansion of Dr Lek Tantasanee.

The heart of the central Siamese house is its broad wooden terrace or *chaan*, around which the cabins are grouped and from which they are entered. From a bird's eye view, this deck is the single largest part of the house, occupying as much as 40% of the floor plan, or 60% if the cabin verandahs are included.

The deck is built about 40 cm lower than the verandah, approximately seat-height, so it forms a kind of built-in bench. The gap between the two levels is often left open, which accounts for its Thai name, *chong maew rod*, meaning 'a cat's gate'. But the gap is meant to let breezes through, not pets, taking advantage of the cooler air from the covered space below the house.

In many houses, a shade tree is planted at ground level to grow up through an opening in the centre of the deck. In the morning and late afternoon, the terrace is shaded by the walls and roofs of the surrounding house cabins, and by the deck's own wooden walls, which are ventilated by balustrades. The shade and sense of enclosure help to turn the deck into a comfortable multi-purpose space for sharing meals, entertaining guests, making handicrafts or other activities.

The house interiors and yard might be bare, but the terrace is often arranged with ceramic vats of ornamental fish and water lilies as well as potted plants. Birds may be kept in cages, sometimes in a special pavilion called a *ho nok*. A big home with three or five house cabins and a broad terrace may have an open pavilion in the middle called a *ho klang*, which is used as a sitting room.

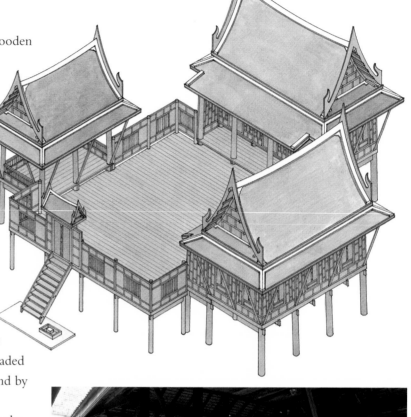

3.10 Steps and Balustrades

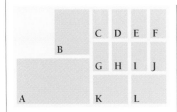

A. A balustrade can simultaneously enclose a space, and open out into its surroundings, as at the villas in the Samui island resort of Le Royal Meridien Baan Taling Ngam.

B. A verandah balustrade doubles as built-in seating at Ayutthaya's Khun Phaen House.

C–F. An assortment of fretted, carved and painted balustrades.

G. Southern homeowners often prefer cement to wood when building stairs, the better to cope with damp ground.

H. In rural districts, steps are made to be retracted at night, to thwart intruders and wild animals.

I. The stairs to this house in Khorat feature seven steps above the landing.

J. Wooden stairs of an old hotel in Phitsanulok province.

K. Wooden fretwork and a timber balustrade lighten up the masonry elements of this old shop building.

L. A ladder of seven rungs reaches the terrace of this tidy northeastern house at the Isaan Village Museum in Kalasin province.

A house elevated on posts needs stairs. The most basic form is a bamboo or wooden ladder that can be retracted at night for protection against intruders and wild animals. A house with a large terrace may have fixed stairs at the front entrance, often with a dog-legged layout and a gable-roofed gate at the top. A smaller, secondary stairway may be built at the rear of the terrace. Stairs and ladders are always built with an uneven number of steps, not including the landing; even-numbered stairways are believed to be steps for ghosts.

The terrace is bordered by timber balustrades and railings that create a sense of enclosure while also admitting breezes and light. In addition to using elements that are sawn, turned or sometimes cut into fretwork designs, there are usually vertical load-bearing supports placed every 1 m or 2 m along the line. Terrace balustrades in central Siamese houses can take a form rather like walls, being quite tall, with narrow rectangular wooden panels in the *fa pakon* style at the top, bottom and sometimes sides of the balustrade section. Balustrades and railings are seen at their most decorative in regional styles: Lanna and Shan houses of the north, and Thai Muslim houses in the south.

3.11 Yards

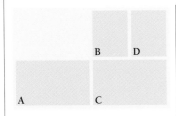

A. *The landscaping of a traditional house is decided less by the rules of good taste than by the wish for good food, good fragrances and good luck.*

B. *A water lily garden decorates the grounds at Sathien Dhamma Sathan meditation centre in Bangkok.*

C. *Daily sweeping keeps the packed earth of the yard free from debris. The cool space under the house gets far more daytime use than the interior does.*

D. *The late M. R. Kukrit Pramoj, a statesman, novelist and aesthete, cultivated gardens in an aristocratic and eclectic Bangkok style.*

The traditional yard is a scrappy affair; the ground around the stilts is often just clay, packed hard by foot traffic. There might be a few bushes, chosen not for their beauty but their resistance to drought and flood. Some households keep potted plants, selected for their auspiciousness or fragrance rather than decorative qualities. Trees may stand around the yard, but usually not directly over the house, which is considered unlucky, except in the case of the terrace shade tree, often planted to grow up through an opening in the centre of the deck.

Other plants are grown in patches for cooking. The kitchen garden (*suan kruah*) sprouts herbs and spices such as lemon grass, chili, galangal and garlic. There may also be a medicinal herb garden (*suan sa-mun-prai*). Plants and trees favoured for their fragrant blossoms include *ma-li* (night blooming jasmine) and *jam-pee* or white *chempaka* (*Michelia alba*), which is used to make ceremonial wreaths. Banana trees are fast-growing favourites.

Plants considered auspicious owe their luck to their good names. The gooseberry tree, or *ma yom*, might make people like you, since it sounds like *ni yom*, meaning popular. If you would rather be feared than loved, plant tamarind, or *ma kham*, since *kham* means 'to be feared'. Put a jack fruit tree (*ka noon*) behind the house if you are looking for support, *noon*.

Trees are situated to mark the boundaries of the compound, which typically range from 200–400 sq m. Certain trees are considered lucky when placed at the right points of the compass around the house. Yards in the south and northeast are often not enclosed by a fence or wall, since relatives tend to inhabit a neighbourhood, turning it into an extended family compound.

As important as the yard itself is the space under the house, which is sheltered from the sun and rain, and is used for rest, making handicrafts and family activities. It can also be used to raise chickens or pigs.

3.12 Wood

A. The Thai house's humble face is unpainted timber.

B & C. A rice barn's studs are built on the outside to form a smooth surface inside to hold the grain neatly.

D–O. Wood proves versatile in such elements as carved decorations, structural components using joinery and surface coverings. The decorative elements of a traditional house are usually limited to reliefs carved in floral lai thai patterns on window panels and roof finials (D, H & J). The wooden pegs and slots of joined elements are better able to withstand stress than nailed or bolted structures (E, M & O). Timber structures stand on cement posts when built in damp localities to better resist rot (F, I, L & N).

The sophistication of the *ruen khrueng sap*, or timber house, reflects the availability of many of the world's best types of wood in Thailand. Some 500 local species of trees have been classified by the government's Forestry Organisation as having commercial value. Forests covered over 80% of the country until the middle of the 20th century, so Thais naturally relied on timber when building permanent structures. These resources became so heavily exploited that logging was banned in 1989, when forests then occupied just 20% of the land.

The most important wood used is teak, or *mai sak* (*tectona grandis*), due to its excellent qualifications for building. The teak tree grows tall and straight, so it can be milled into a maximum amount of quality wood. It contains sap that gives it resistance to insects and fungus, helping teak houses last up to 200 years.

Another versatile wood is narra, or *pradu* (*pterocarpus macroarpus*), a hard, medium-weight timber with a yellow colouration. Moderate in cost, it is used for structural elements, interior finish, panelling and furniture.

Several varieties of rosewood (*dalbergia*) are used too. Siamese rosewood, or *payung* (*d. cochinchinensis*), is used for Chinese furniture, as is tamalin, or *ching chan* (*d. dongnaiensis*), known as the 'king of wood'.

Monkey pod tree, or *maka mong* (*afzelia xylocarpa*), is a strong, heavy wood used in floors, stairs, furniture, beams, window and door frames, panelling and veneer.

Malabar ironwood, or *thakien thong* (*hopea odorata*), is a huge tree used widely in construction.

Gurjan, or *yang na* (*dipterocarpus alatus*), is widely used in structural elements, interiors, frames, furniture and plywood.

3.13 Bamboo and Thatch

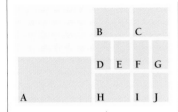

A. A Shan house in the Muang Pon district of Mae Hong Son province.

B. A Shan woman sews leathery *tong tung* leaves onto slats that will be layered onto a roof frame, starting from the base of the roof, moving up.

C. The underside of the thatched *tong tung* roof shows neat craftsmanship.

D. Grass, reeds or palm leaves are sewn onto slats of bamboo or rattan before being layered onto the roof.

E & G. Bangkok Airways' airport at Sukhothai has won recognition for its use of vernacular bamboo construction

F. The firm's Samui Airport employs a thatched roof on a timber frame.

H. Split bamboo makes for lightweight panels almost as sturdy as wood.

I. Rattan and split bamboo both make for precise weaving.

J. Simple reed matting of the sort used for wall panels.

The primordial materials used in Thai house construction are thatch for the roof covering and bamboo for almost any element. Bamboo is nature's gift to builders—fast-growing, easily harvested, lightweight, strong and flexible. It is so versatile that the bamboo house, or *ruen khrueng phook*, can be made almost entirely from this material alone. Householders can build a bamboo house themselves, without help from craftsmen. The pieces are interlocked using joinery or bound together with fibres made from vines, palm leaves, rattan or crushed young bamboo stems. Bamboo can also be used in combination with wood, relegating timber to structural elements like posts and beams.

Of the world's 1,200 species of bamboo, about 60 flourish in Thailand. Supplies of wild bamboo have been reduced by deforestation and mismanaged harvesting, so it is increasingly being cultivated. Harvested after two or three years, the stems are treated with heat, water or chemicals to protect against insects and fungus. Stems can be used whole, halved, quartered, or in cuts as fine as string. Split in half and flattened, it can be used to make a plank-like surface for benches and flooring.

Of the many types of grasses and tree leaves that Thais use as roof thatch, the most popular is mangrove palm or nipa palm, called *chak* (*Nypa fruticans*), which grows along the banks of canals and rivers. Vetiver grass, or *ya-faek* (*Vetiveria zizanioides*), makes a good roof covering thanks to its waxy, water-resistant surface, its pleasant aroma and resistance to insects. An architectural emblem of northern Thailand is the beautifully rustic thatch made from the huge leaves of a tree called *tong tung*, a species of dipterocarpus related to *yang*, or garjan. Other thatch materials include banana leaves, sago palm leaves (*Metroxylon sagu*), sugar palm bark (*Arenga saccarifera*) and elephant grass (*Pennisetum purpureum*).

3.14 Construction

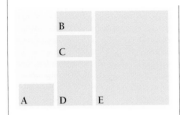

A. The roof's wooden structure is pre-assembled before being hoisted above the cabin and fitted with tiles.

B. The Thai house lacks a ceiling, which means the roof can be repaired from the inside. Gaps in the truss help to ventilate hot air.

C. The use of joinery fittings rather than nails allows posts, beams and other elements to be easily disassembled and reused.

D. Walls of the northern house lean out towards the roof.

E. The Thai house is essentially a machine for living made from a kit. Each part has a structural function and name.

For all its simple charm, the wooden Thai house requires specialists to be built, both a master carpenter and a Brahmin priest or astrologer to determine an auspicious time and location for the project.

Construction starts at the builder's shop, where the components are carpentered before they are transported to the site. Once a lucky position for the house is selected, holes are dug for the posts and fitted with wooden bases to prevent sinking. A ceremonial raising of the first post begins the job, preceded by the chanting of monks, a blessing of the post with lustral water, and the placement of pieces of nine auspicious types of wood in the post hole. The remaining posts are raised one by one, going in a clockwise direction.

Next comes the construction of the roof elements, then walls and finally the floor. Elements were traditionally joined using wooden pegs, but metal bolts and nails are now often used. The job takes about a dozen workers, formerly neighbourhood volunteers supervised by the carpenter, but nowadays usually done on hire.

Ritual aspects are as important and complex as the technical methods of construction itself. A post, for example, must not be oozing sap, and its knots must not be of certain types or in certain positions. Even the position in which the post lies on the ground before being raised must follow guidelines determined by the month. Additional rules govern the size, proportions and materials of other components as well as plantings in the yard.

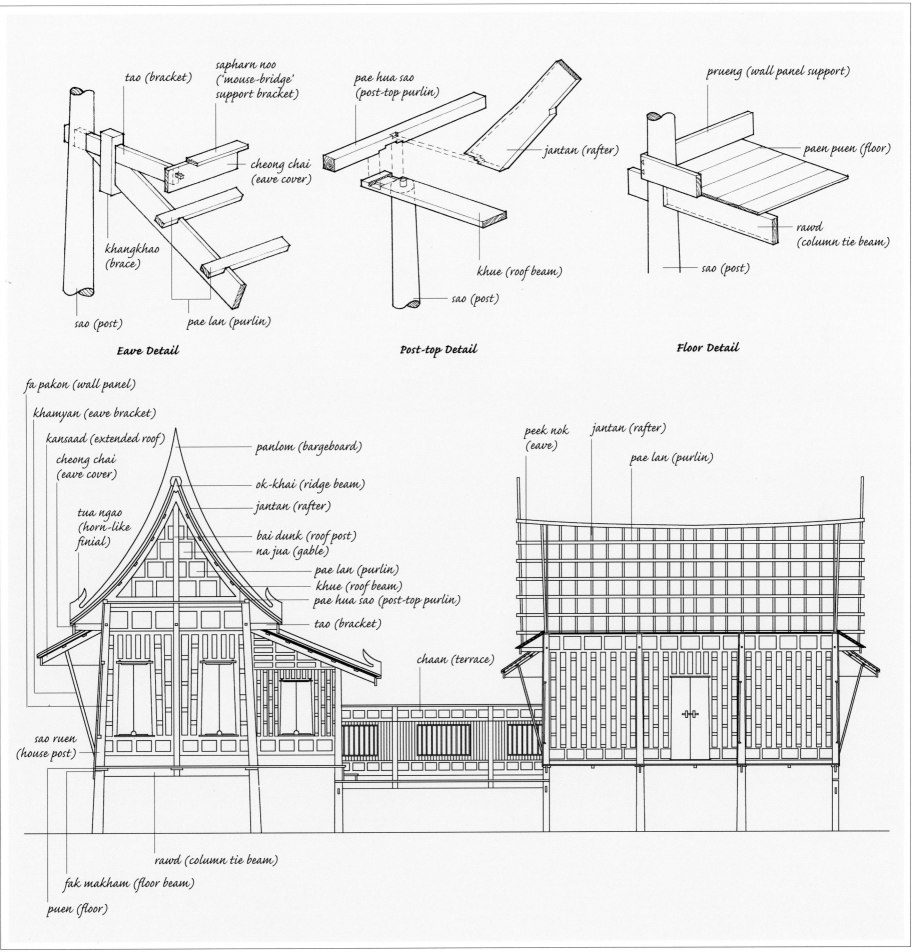

tao (bracket)

sapharn noo
('mouse-bridge'
support bracket)

cheong chai
(eave cover)

khangkhao
(brace)

sao (post)

pae lan (purlin)

Eave Detail

pae hua sao
(post-top purlin)

jantan (rafter)

khue (roof beam)

sao (post)

Post-top Detail

prueng (wall panel support)

paen puen (floor)

rawd
(column tie beam)

sao (post)

Floor Detail

fa pakon (wall panel)

khamyan (eave bracket)

kansaad (extended roof)

cheong chai
(eave cover)

tua ngao
(horn-like
finial)

panlom (bargeboard)

ok-khai (ridge beam)

jantan (rafter)

bai dunk (roof post)

na jua (gable)

pae lan (purlin)

khue (roof beam)

pae hua sao (post-top purlin)

tao (bracket)

peek nok
(eave)

jantan (rafter)

pae lan (purlin)

chaan (terrace)

sao ruen
(house post)

rawd (column tie beam)

fak makham (floor beam)

puen (floor)

Religious Architecture

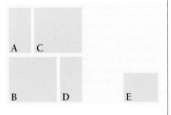

Thais observe the most conservative form of Buddhism, Theravada. It is a religion of cultivated dispassion, yet it has inspired a passion to build, which is reflected in both the large number of temples in Thailand—some 30,000—and in their architectural spirit. They suggest visions of the celestial, with multiple layers of form and ornament that turn a temple hall into a kind of palace for the Buddha images housed within. In the national architectural hierarchy, temples stand higher even than palaces. Until the Ayutthaya period, only temples were allowed to be built with the permanent materials of stone, brick and stucco, while palaces were built with wood.

Before modern times, Siamese rulers built large temples in their cities not only to make merit, but also to strengthen their domains. A temple enshrining an important relic, for instance, would attract people to live in its vicinity because they wished to be protected by its spiritual power. As a result, the government there benefited from having a bigger populace from which to obtain labour and taxes.

Temple architecture is governed by the influence of centuries of tradition and by official guidelines set by the Department of Religious Affairs. Yet architects and craftspeople find scope for innovation within these limits. Over the course of the last millennium, Thai temple architecture has absorbed influences from India, Ceylon, Burma, Cambodia, China, Persia and Europe. Regional variations within Thailand are symbols of the nation's own cultural diversity. Thai temples are opulent and regal in the central region; gracefully sinuous in the north; rustic and charming in the northeast; and in the south, sometimes quite eclectic.

Diversity is also apparent in Thailand's 3,000 mosques, which can be seen in most large towns. They are centres of religious and social life for diverse Muslim communities of both Thai and immigrant origin. The coexistence of Islam with Buddhism is reflected in the architecture of mosques that resemble Buddhist chapels, and Buddhist chapels that resemble mosques. Several of the mosques in Thailand's deep south, where Muslims are a majority, are among the most unique and architecturally significant examples of Islamic worship sites in Southeast Asia.

A. The ho trai *at Chiang Mai's Wat Phra Singh—the finest in the north.*

B. *The assembly hall and chedi of Wat Phra That Chae Haeng in Nan date to the 14th century.*

C. *Chiang Rai's Wat Phra Kaeo is where the green jasper sculpture known as the Emerald Buddha was discovered.*

D. *Ayutthaya's religious architecture, as seen at Wat Na Phra Men, shaped the design of temples in Rattanakosin.*

E. *Burmese influence shows in the chedis and seven-tiered roofs of Wat Chong Kham and Wat Chong Klang in Mae Hong Son.*

Preceding pages: The Thai chedi is a form that evolved in Ceylon over 600 years ago from ancient Indian memorial burial mounds.

4.1 The Temple Compound

The Thai Buddhist temple, or *wat*, is not a building but a place, a complex that serves as a community centre for religious rites, learning, social life, recreation and even festivals. The *wat* is also a small community in itself, since almost every *wat* is also a monastery.

White courtyard walls and decorated gates announce the compound's holy status. Its layout, moreover, follows a sacred design—a formal ground plan that contrasts with the impromptu sprawl of the village or city. Viewed from the sky, as a deity might view it, the ground plan outlines a sacred diagram, or *mandala*, a structure influenced by Khmer-Hindu temples. Buildings are arranged in a series of zones, with a succession of increasingly sacred, walled layers centring on the ordination hall, or *ubosot*, where the holiest rites transpire. This is the heart of the *wat's* ceremonial grounds, or *phutthawat*, which are enclosed within their own special courtyard walls, or *kampaeng kaew*.

The complex is geographically aligned, starting from the ordination hall, whose entrance side faces east. Next to it are one or more assembly halls, or *viharn*, housing Buddha images and murals. There may be a memorial tower in the form of a bell-shaped stupa known as a *chedi*, or a bullet-shaped *prang*. The grounds may contain cloisters, which are covered galleries open on one side to display Buddha figures.

Other elements are the scripture pavilion (*ho trai*), study hall (*sala kan parian*) and bell tower (*ho rakhang*). Monks inhabit their own zone, the *sanghawat*, with cabins known as *kuti*, a dining hall, libraries and other facilities for monastic life.

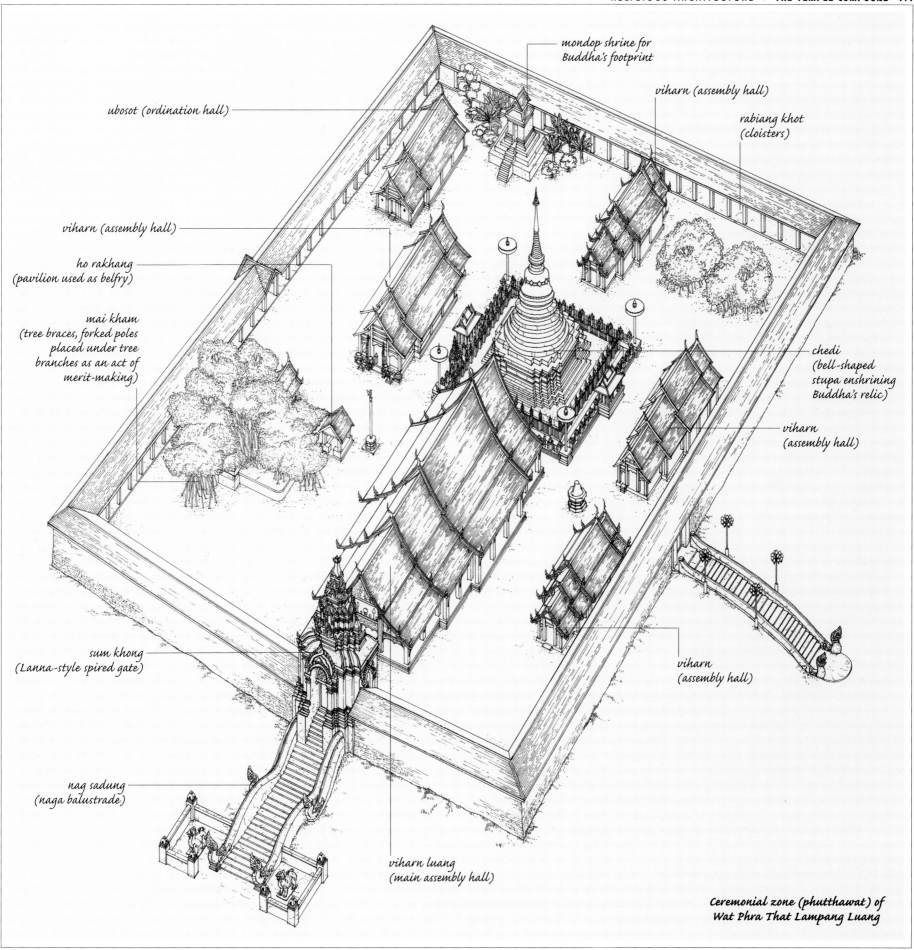

mondop shrine for
Buddha's footprint

viharn (assembly hall)

rabiang khot
(cloisters)

ubosot (ordination hall)

viharn (assembly hall)

ho rakhang
(pavilion used as belfry)

mai kham
(tree braces, forked poles
placed under tree
branches as an act of
merit-making)

chedi
(bell-shaped
stupa enshrining
Buddha's relic)

viharn
(assembly hall)

sum khong
(Lanna-style spired gate)

viharn
(assembly hall)

nag sadung
(naga balustrade)

viharn luang
(main assembly hall)

Ceremonial zone (phutthawat) of
Wat Phra That Lampang Luang

4.2 Ordination Halls and Assembly Halls

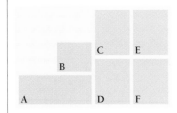

A. Bangkok's Wat Benchamabophit, designed by King Rama V's brother Prince Naris in 1899. The King wrote to the prince, 'I never flatter anyone but I cannot help saying that you captured my heart in accomplishing such beauty as this.'

B. The viharn of Wat Nong Daeng, a Thai Lue temple in Nan, built in 1878, exudes a plainspoken grace.

C. The cloistered assembly hall of Bangkok's royal Wat Suthat stands on a double plinth, with a verandah and triple entrance based on Ayutthaya models. Encircling the chapel are 28 Chinese pagodas symbolising the 28 Buddhas born on earth.

D. The viharn of Wat Sao Tong Thong in Lopburi is believed to have been founded as a Christian church or mosque in the 16th century. It was later converted into a Buddhist temple.

E. The 1628 ubosot of Nakhon Sri Thammarat's Wat Mahathat. Note the slanting columns and projecting gable.

F. The viharn of Wat Tha Kham in Chiang Mai's Mae Malai village.

Following pages: The viharn of Chiang Mai's Wat Ton Kwen (or Wat Inthrawat) is surrounded on three sides by cloisters. Built in 1858, it stands beside a sala in mondop form, used annually during a procession of Buddha relics that traverses the province.

Each *wat* has just a single chapel where monks are ordained, the *ubosot*, the most important building in the compound. Standing on sacred ground which is outlined by eight consecrated boundary markers, this ordination hall is typically a symphony of forms, figures, finishes and colours, decorated on almost every surface except its whitewashed outside walls.

Built on one storey with a rectangular floor plan and a raised plinth, the *ubosot* has a high ceiling and a steep, multi-tiered gable roof with stylised finials at the ridge and eaves. Its doors are covered in carved wood or plaster relief, gold leaf, glass mosaic, lacquer painting or mother-of-pearl inlay.

Tall windows line both lateral walls, with timber doors at the narrow entrance end, facing east. Across from the entrance door at the west end of the interior is the *ubosot's* largest Buddha statue, placed behind a multi-tiered altar. The altar's splendour is matched by painted murals on all four walls depicting Hindu divinities, the Buddha's life story and past lives of the Buddha.

The term *ubosot*, shortened to *bot* in Thai colloquial speech, is derived from the Pali term *uposathagara*, which refers to a hall used for rituals on the *upostha* days—the Buddhist Sabbath, which falls four times a month on the full moon, new moon

and eighth day after each. On these days, monks gather to confess if they have broken any of the 227 precepts of monastic conduct.

The assembly hall, or *viharn*, is architecturally similar but lacks boundary markers, and there may be more than one in the *wat* compound. It is used for sermons and ceremonies involving monks and lay people, and houses Buddha images.

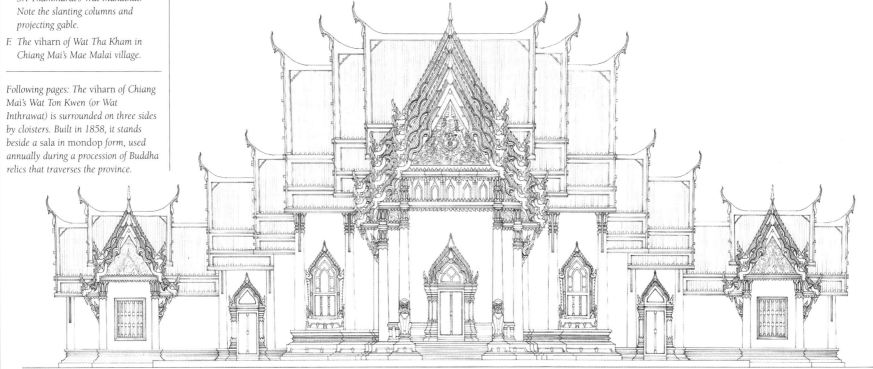

82

4.3 Boundary Markers

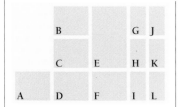

A. A boundary marker on a pedestal with clustered lotus blossom mouldings at Ayutthaya's late 17th-century Wat Salapun.

B. Boundary markers stand around the ubosot at the four cardinal points of the compass and the four points in between.

C. The ubosot of Wat Bhodi Chai in Kalasin province stands in humble contrast to its boundary markers in their elaborate spired mondops.

D. The design of spired mondops housing boundary markers at Bangkok's Wat Saket was inspired by the curved roofs of howdahs, the seats used on elephants. The double bai sema, visible in the middle shrine, indicates the temple's royal sponsorship.

E. The most elaborate of all boundary markers stands in the gilded mondops of the Temple of the Emerald Buddha, with quadruple spires, three-tiered bases and glass mosaic.

F. Gilded luk nimit stand on display in the courtyard of Bangkok's Wat Pathum in 2005, awaiting installation at a Thai-sponsored temple to be built in Kaya, India.

G. Boundary markers at Bangkok's Wat Thepthidaram, founded by King Rama III in the 1830s.

H. Markers at Wat Mahannopharam in Bangkok.

I. Boundary markers at Roi Et province's Wat Rasisalai.

J. At Bangkok's royal Wat Boworniwet, boundary markers are incorporated into the ubosot's wall.

K. Prang-spired mondops house markers at Wat Daowadeungsaram in Thonburi.

L. A boundary marker mounted on a lotus petal cluster platform standing on a lion's throne base dating to the Ayutthaya period, at Phitsanulok's Wat Ratchaburana.

The construction of an ordination hall begins with the ceremonial burial of special stones called *luk nimit* in the surrounding courtyard at the four cardinal points of the compass and four points in between. A ninth stone is buried under the floor in the centre of the hall or under the main Buddha image, thus marking the geographic centre of the whole temple compound.

Standing above the ground where the eight stones are buried are boundary markers, or *bai sema*. These markers designate the sacred grounds where monks' ceremonies, such as confession and ordination rites, may take place. The markers may only be installed with government permission.

Boundary markers can take many forms, usually a tablet shaped like the leaf of a Bodhi tree. Typically made of stone or plaster, the markers are often enclosed in small shrines. They are also often built in double form, placed back-to-back, or even tripled. This indicates that the hall was consecrated a second time, such as upon a major renovation, or that it enjoys royal sponsorship. At a few temples, the markers are enclosed within the columns of the *ubosot* or its courtyard wall. The boundary markers of country temples may simply be boulders, or even living trees.

4.4 Pavilions and Sermon Halls

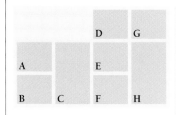

A. *The interior of an open-air* sala kan parian *at Thonburi's Wat Hong Rattanaram.*

B. *Chinese-style roofs distinguish the pavilions at Thonburi's Wat Arun.*

C. *A pavilion at Bangkok's Wat Rachathiwat, in the neo-Khmer style developed by Prince Naris, who renovated the monastery during the Fifth Reign.*

D. *A mondop-style* sala *that serves as a boat landing at Wat Choltara Singhae in the deep south province of Narathiwat.*

E. *Prince Naris modelled the* sala kan parian *at Bangkok's Wat Rajathiwat on the sermon hall at the Ayutthaya-period Wat Yai Suwannaram in Phetchburi. Built of teak, with arched windows of neo-Gothic or Moorish inspiration, the hall can accommodate 1,000 people.*

F. *A* sala *that shelters a bell and resting monks at Wat Phra That Lampang Luang in Lampang.*

G. *A* sala kan parian *at Wat Tah Phrya in the Pak Panung district of Nakhon Sri Thammarat.*

H. *A cruciform* sala *at Bangkok's Wat Benchamabophit houses a northern-style long drum and Chinese-style bell.*

The courtyards of *wats* often feature one or more open-air pavilions, or *sala*, built as places for visitors and monks to hold meetings, rest, meditate or have meals while sheltered from the sun and rain. Thais like to make merit by sponsoring the construction of *salas*, so few temples suffer from a shortage.

The layout of a *sala* usually follows the rectangular format of an assembly hall, using a gabled roof that is less elaborate. It tends to be built entirely or partly without walls. Indeed, the open-air *sala* might be viewed as the primordial form of the temple hall since, in the traditions of the old Sukhothai and Lanna kingdoms, assembly halls and ordination halls were often built that way. A few examples still stand.

The highest form of the temple *sala* is the study hall, also known as the sermon hall, preaching hall or *sala kan parian*.

This pavilion is traditionally built as a hall in which clerics can instruct lay people in Buddhist doctrine, and is sometimes also used as a place for monks to chant and perform ceremonies. A *sala kan parian* may be as large as an assembly hall, or even larger, and partly or fully enclosed by walls.

Parian refers to a system of formal examination for monastic study; a degree system introduced in the 18th century by King Narai. Its highest level took nine years of study. Thus, the name of the hall suggests seriousness of intent in learning, even if one is just listening to a sermon.

The elementary or secondary school facilities that are built on the grounds of many *wats* are not, however, *sala kan parian*, which are better thought of as preaching halls than as secular classrooms.

4.5 Cloisters

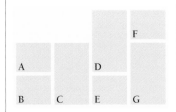

A. Cloisters at Nakhon Sri Thammarat's Wat Mahathat. Lay people visit this part of a temple to pay their respects to the Buddha images housed within.

B. Cloisters at Wat Khian Bang Kaeo in Phatthalung province.

C. At Bangkok's sublime Wat Benchamabophit, the cloisters house dozens of Buddhas from different periods standing on pedestals designed by the wat's architect, Prince Naris. The seven Buddhas seen in this photo each represent a different day of the week. One makes offerings to the Buddha corresponding to the day of the week on which he or she was born.

D. Walls of the gallery at Bangkok's royal Wat Rachabophit are decorated in glazed ceramic tiles.

E. Curving cloister at Phra Pathom Chedi in Nakhon Pathom.

F. As at many temples, the cloisters surrounding the magnificent viharn of Bangkok's Wat Suthat are often busy with monks teaching classes or gatherings for ordinations and other ceremonies.

G. The arcade surrounding the chedi at Thonburi's Wat Prayun has a Roman mood. The chedi enshrines the ashes of members of the Bunnag family.

At major temples, courtyards around the key structure, whether ordination hall, assembly hall, *chedi* or *prang*, are often encompassed by cloisters. Called *phra rabiang khot*, or simply *rabiang khot*, these are covered walkways or galleries with one open side along which the roof is supported by pillars. The inner wall displays Buddha statues or murals. Despite its resemblance to the cloisters of Christian monasteries, this structure was derived from the fully enclosed stone cloisters built around Khmer sanctuaries such as Prasat Phimai and Prasat Phnom Rung.

As part of the *wat's* cosmological ground plan, cloisters represent one of the layers of mountains or oceans around Mount Meru, which is symbolised by the encircled building. In Ayutthaya-era temple layouts, the *chedi* or *prang* was the central temple structure. During the Rattanakosin period, the ordination hall or the assembly hall often became the key structure built within cloisters. In both periods, the importance of the building depended on the significance of the relic or Buddha image housed within the structure.

The cloistered area is typically where holiday circumambulation rites take place, allowing worshippers to contemplate the enclosed Buddha images as they proceed. In many temples, cloisters also provide a sheltered space in which monks can conduct classes.

Of all Thailand's cloisters, the most exceptional can be found at the Grand Palace, where a vast length of galleries surround the entire complex of the Temple of the Emerald Buddha. Unlike most cloisters, these do not house Buddha images, but 178 panels of murals illustrating the entire Ramakian tales—the Thai version of the Hindu Ramayana epic that recounts the adventures of Rama, the earthly incarnation of the Hindu god Vishnu. The murals are an homage to the Thai king because monarchs of the Chakri dynasty are regarded as incarnations of Rama.

4.6 The *Prang* Memorial Tower

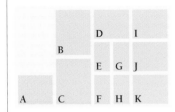

A. *The Khmer prang, such as the 12th-century Prasat Phnom Rung in Buri Ram, has a sanctuary entered by telescoping antechambers, or a mandapa. These were shortened to small porches or niches in the Thai prang that evolved later.*

B. *During the Ayutthaya era, the prang evolved into a tall, bullet-shaped structure integrating base, body and tower. Illustrated here is the prang of Sukhothai's Wat Mahathat Chaliang, built in 1475.*

C. *Sealed in 1424 and opened in 1957, the prang of Ayutthaya's Wat Ratchaburana revealed three levels of chambers lined by murals and filled with some 600 Buddha images, 100,000 votive tablets, royal regalia, and other precious items.*

D. *Ayutthaya kings built prangs at Wat Mahathat and many other sites after Siam's conquest of the Khmer empire.*

E. *One of the few prangs in the north, at Wat Suan Tan in Nan province.*

F. *Phitsanulok province's Wat Mahathat has a central tower erected in 1337 as a lotus bud chedi which was renovated into a prang in Ayutthaya times, then covered in gold mosaic during the reign of King Rama V.*

G. *The prang of Ayutthaya's Wat Chai Watthanaram, built in 1630, is surrounded by eight smaller prangs in a Khmer-influenced layout that later shaped Thonburi's Wat Arun.*

H. *This red prang lies at Phra Nakhon Kiri, King Rama IV's palace in Phetchburi province, built in 1858.*

I. *The curving form of the Khmer prang built in Khorat at Prasat Phimai influenced the architecture of Angkor Wat and Thailand.*

J. *Dating to 1374, Ayutthaya's Wat Mahathat was one of the capital's largest temples and residence of the Supreme Patriarch.*

K. *A Rattanakosin prang: the tower of Thonburi's Wat Arun, or Temple of Dawn, is an emblem of Bangkok.*

The imposing structure of the *prang*, often surrounded by open cloisters, is a form inherited from the pre-Tai era of the 6th through to the 12th centuries, when Khmer dominions extended into much of what is now central and northeastern Thailand. The Khmers first built their Brahman sanctuaries in the pyramidal form of Indian *sikhara*. In the 11th and 12th centuries, however, the *sikhara* form evolved into the curving, bullet shape of the *prang* at both Brahman and Mahayana Buddhist sites. Sukhothai-era Thais later adopted the *prang* for use as a Theravada Buddhist relic chamber.

Both the *sikhara* and *prang* have 33 levels—bases, tiers, mouldings and finial—that represent the 33 levels of Mount Meru in Hindu cosmology. In the Mahayana and later Theravada towers, these came to signify the 33 levels of perfection outlined by Buddhist doctrine.

The *prang's* bullet-shaped top is formed underneath by tiers of receding cubes. This geometry is given its curve by the use of miniature gables and antefixes, or corner pieces, that curve inward towards their tops. The rectangular body of the structure is visually integrated with the curving top by the use of tall gables above the entrance. Thais built these monuments in brick or laterite covered with stucco rather than the carved sandstone preferred by Khmer builders east of the Mekong.

The sacred relics enshrined in *prangs* (and stupas or *chedis*) are often cremation ashes, in a few cases believed to be from the Buddha or a disciple. Some *prangs* encase the ashes of a monarch or revered monk. A relic chamber may also hold Buddhist inscriptions or an image, such as a Buddha footprint.

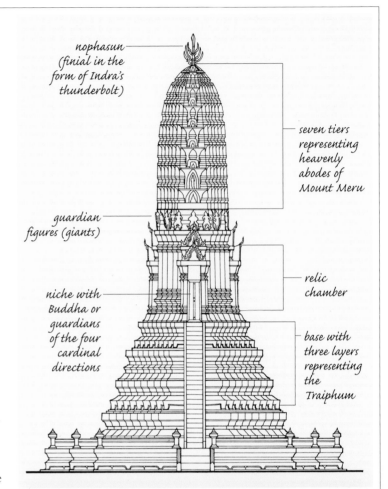

nophasun (finial in the form of Indra's thunderbolt)

seven tiers representing heavenly abodes of Mount Meru

guardian figures (giants)

relic chamber

niche with Buddha or guardians of the four cardinal directions

base with three layers representing the Traiphum

4.7 The *Chedi* Memorial Tower

A. From left: Chiang Mai's Chedi Liam, built in 1288, emulating Lamphun's Mon chedi; Chedi Chet Yod was built in the 15th century for the World Buddhist Council held in Chiang Mai; in the 16th century, the round, bell-shaped chedi configuration was transformed by redentation from base to spire, as at Ayutthaya's Sri Suriyothai; the Laotian-style Phra That Phanom in Nakhon Phanom has four curved sides; and Sri Satchanalai's 14th-century Chedi Chet Thaeo.

B. The chedi of Ayutthaya's Wat Yai Chaimongkhol has a tall, octagonal, three-tiered base.

C. Chiang Mai's Chedi Prong was influenced by Yunannese or Mon Hariphunchai pagodas.

D. The diminishing spheres of Chiang Mai's Yunnanese-influenced Wat Kutao represent five Buddhas.

E. The 1492 Ceylonese-style chedi of Ayutthaya's royal Wat Sri Sanphet.

F. A Sukhothai-style chedi at Chiang Mai's Wat Umong.

G. Lamphun's Wat Phra That Hariphunchai has a Mon pyramidal chedi built before the 13th century.

H. Nakhon Sri Thammarat's Wat Mahathat has a 75-m-tall chedi built in 1176 over a pyramidal chedi erected in the 8th century or before.

I. A Lanna chedi.

J. A 19th-century chedi at Thonburi's Wat Arun is redented from base through the spire.

K. The chedi at Phayao's Wat Sri Umong Kham.

L. The chedi at Songkhla's Wat Cha Thing Phra was built over a Srivijaya stupa erected in 999.

M. Phra That Phanom, built in 1539 on a 10th-century Mon chedi.

N. In Lamphun, Wat Phra That Hariphunchai's Lanna-style chedi has a high redented square base, with triple, circular plinths below the bell.

Temples may feature one or more stupas, or memorial towers, usually in the conical form called a *chedi*. This name is based on the word *chetiya* in the Pali language of Theravada scripture, which refers to a burial mound or pyre. From ancient times, Indians built mounds to memorialise deceased leaders; such stupas were built to enshrine relics of the Buddha.

Buddhist stupas began to be built in Thailand in the central region of the Chao Phraya River basin in the 7th century or earlier by Theravada Mons. These early stupas are believed to have been built in a dome-like form influenced by Indian models. The later Mon chiefdom of Hariphunchai, in what is now Lamphun, built pyramid-shaped stupas. A few examples built during or before the 13th century survive.

Thailand's predominant *chedi* type is the bell-shaped form introduced during the Sukhothai era which was influenced by Ceylonese models, perhaps via Burma or Nakhon Sri Thammarat. The Siamese version evolved towards an ever taller and more slender shape.

The *chedi* has three levels: a base, a middle section that contains the chamber holding relics, and a top level comprising a spire and its platform. Thai *chedis* are typically built of laterite blocks or brick, decorated with stucco, and stylised by redented geometry in the base, middle, top or throughout. A few have been built on top of older *chedis* or *prangs*. Many Rattanakosin-era *chedis* are clad in gilding, copper or ceramic tiles. Like the *prang*, the *chedi* is a cosmological evocation of Mount Meru.

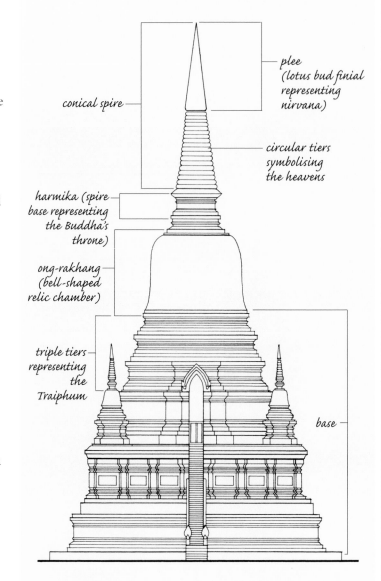

plee (lotus bud finial representing nirvana)

conical spire

circular tiers symbolising the heavens

harmika (spire base representing the Buddha's throne)

ong-rakhang (bell-shaped relic chamber)

triple tiers representing the Traiphum

base

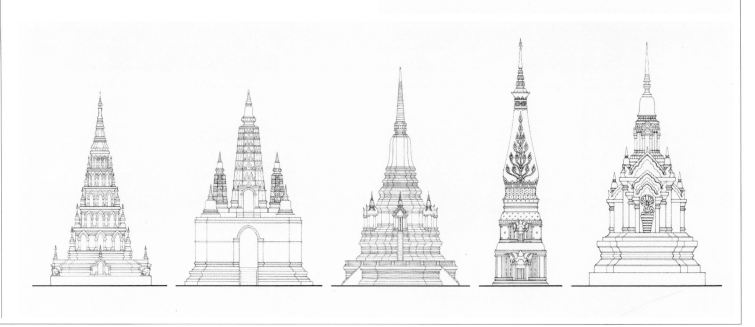

4.8 Monks' Houses

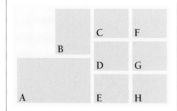

A. *European-influenced kutis at Bangkok's Wat Benchamabophit. Visible in the distance is a 1902 palace that has become a secondary school affiliated with the temple, painted in pink, the colour associated with Tuesday, the day of the week on which King Rama V was born.*

B. *A European-style abbot's residence or library at Bangkok's Wat Buranasiri.*

C. *Thai and Western styles merge in Wat Boworniwet's Tamnak Phet, built in 1913 by King Rama VI as a throne hall for the Supreme Patriarch, head of Siam's monastic order. It continues to function as a conference hall for the top monastic council. King Rama IV served as abbot of the temple before he was crowned.*

D. *King Rama IV spent part of his long monkhood at Bangkok's riverside Wat Rachathiwat.*

E. *Kutis at Bangkok's Wat Mahannopharam.*

F. *Kuti at Wat Thai Yo, on the island of Ko Yoh in the southern province of Songkhla.*

G. *A wooden building that serves as a lavatory in the monk's quarters of Wat Yai Suwanarram, in Phetchburi province.*

H. *Kutis built as a Siamese cluster house, at Phetchburi's Wat Yai Suwannaram.*

The *wat's* main function is to serve as a monastery, a residence for some of the nation's more than 300,000 monks and novices. Almost all active Thai temples have resident monks, except the Temple of the Emerald Buddha in the Grand Palace, which is reserved for royal use.

The monks' private residential zone at the back or side of the compound contains houses called *kuti*, usually small wooden or white plastered brick buildings, each with a single upstairs room and ground floor. Monks' houses are scattered around the zone and are interconnected by walkways that also lead to shared facilities such as bathrooms and a Pali language school. In a few monasteries, the *kutis* are built as a cluster house on posts with a central terrace.

The monks dine in a large building with a high ceiling, often constructed without walls for the sake of ventilation. There is also usually at least one other pavilion, or *sala*, for the monks to gather to meditate or pray. In a small temple, a single hall will serve dual functions as a place to eat and meditate.

4.9 Scripture Pavilions

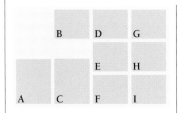

The ceremonial zone or residential zone for monks also features a small but sacred repository or library called a *ho trai*, which houses Buddhist scriptures. It is a place for monks to study, but it has a symbolic role as well, standing as a kind of shrine to Buddhist doctrine, or *dhamma*. This is because it shelters copies of the early texts called the Tripitaka, which originated from the Buddha's sermons and are the foundation of the Theravada branch of Buddhism that is practiced in Thailand.

The *ho trai* is usually built in either of two forms that show its sacred status. Often, it resembles an assembly hall in miniature, with a rectangular floor plan, verandah, multi-tiered roof and ornamented gables. In other instances, it assumes the square or cruciform structure of the *mondop* (see 4.11 The *Mondop*). Most temples have only a single *ho trai*; very large temples might have more.

The *ho trai* was traditionally constructed of wood and set on tall posts placed in the middle of a pond; a graceful structural form designed for protection against termites

and floods. With just one or two windows and a single door, the only access to the *ho trai* was via a tall ladder that could be removed to discourage thieves.

Limits on the space available for temples built in the past half century or so have often required the *ho trai* pond to be omitted. In such cases, the structure can be built on two levels instead (see photo H), with a brick-and-mortar lower level that prevents termites from reaching the upper level of wood. Sometimes the *ho trai* is simply built on one level directly on the ground, with a high cement base (see photo G).

4.10 Drum Towers and Bell Towers

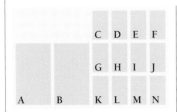

A. A drum tower in an unusual variation of the mondop form, at Bangkok's Wat Rachathiwat.

B. In Bangkok's Chinatown, a mondop-style drum tower at Wat Phlapphla Chai.

C. A bronze gong housed in the tower of Wat Phra That Hariphunchai in Lamphun.

D. At Bangkok's Wat Benchamabophit, the main bell tower stands in a lawn in the middle of the monk's zone.

E. The spired roof of the bell tower at Wat Photharam, in the northeastern province of Kalasin, is in a cruciform gabled form.

F. A European-influenced bell tower at Wat Boworniwet in Bangkok.

G. A European-style tower houses the bell at Wat Buranasiri in Bangkok. The construction is new, but its design matches another tower there from the 19th century.

H. The bell tower at Wat Sawang-Arom in Kamphaeng Phet province.

I. The Western-influenced spired bell tower at Wat Yai Suwannaram in Phetchburi province. Such designs often date to the mid-19th century, when Thai architects started adapting Western forms from architecture illustrated in imported books and drawings.

J. A bell tower at the mid-19th century Wat Thung Sri Muang in Ubon Ratchathani.

K. A pavilion at Bangkok's Wat Benchamabophit houses this Chinese-style bell and a northern-style long drum.

L. A rustic bell tower in a provincial temple.

M. Splendid proportions show in the ho rakhang at Wat Mahathat in the northeastern province of Yasothon.

N. The bell tower at the Temple of the Emerald Buddha in the Grand Palace is built in mondop form.

Thai temple architecture includes a traditional form of public address system: a tall tower housing a drum (*ho klong*) or bell (*ho rakhang*) that is struck to announce the hour, the start of religious ceremonies and emergencies. The tower is typically built near the residences of the monks, who do the ringing or drumming.

This tower or belfry usually adopts a square shape and is built on two or three levels. It can have any of several types of roof, including the conventional gable roof or the cross-shaped, four-gable top called *chaturamuk* which is used on royal pavilions or a palace spire.

In rural temples, the towers are usually built of wood, on four round pillars. Some include verandahs with balustrade fretwork done in a folk style. Bangkok temples and those under royal sponsorship have enclosed towers of brick and cement with interior staircases and large window openings to better broadcast sound. They may be decorated with plaster relief or Chinese ceramic tiles, and often have windows and roof structures in Western styles.

The tower is the temple's tallest structure after the *chedi* or *prang*, ordination hall and assembly hall. Height helps the sound of the bell or drum travel beyond the temple to the surrounding community, allowing the instrument to be used as a public clock, announcing village meetings or sounding the alarm for a fire or attack. Within the compound, the signal marks times such as the noon hour, when the monks' day-long fast begins, and the end of the day, when evening prayers start.

The drum used in such towers is of the long type, which rests horizontally on a stand or in a sling. Bells may be made of wood, stone or bronze.

4.11 The *Mondop*

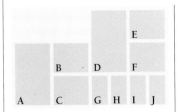

A. Thailand's most magnificent mondop is the Phra Mondop scripture pavilion at the Temple of the Emerald Buddha. It houses the first version of the Tripitaka revised during the Rattanakosin era, the Royal Golden Edition, commissioned by King Rama I early in his reign.

B. The timber scripture pavilion of Wat Choltara Singhae in the southern province of Narathiwat.

C. Lanna and Burmese art merge in the cruciform mondop at Lampang's Wat Pong Sanuk Tai, which houses four Buddha images.

D. The mondop-style courtyard gate at Bangkok's royal Wat Thepsirin has a mongkut- or crown-spired roof.

E. Many of Sukhothai's monumental Buddha images are housed in brick mondops such as the great Phra Attharot at Wat Mahathat.

F. The mondop of Sukhothai's Wat Traphang Thong Long enshrines a Buddha footprint.

G. This mondop reliquary at Bangkok's Wat Thepsirin has a mongkut-spired roof matching the gate nearby (see photo D). It enshrines the ashes of temple donors.

H. Built by King Rama III and decorated with crockery mosaic, this mondop at Thonburi's Wat Arun contains a Buddha footprint.

I. At Bangkok's royal Wat Rachabophit, most of the shrines housing the ashes of royalty are built in variations of the mondop form, including several in Western style.

J. The exquisite Prasat Yod Prang, a ho trai at Wat Rachapradit, is better classed as a prang-spired mondop than a prang per se. Rattanakosin architects innovated a neo-Khmer style incorporating ancient structural and ornamental forms much as 18th- and 19th-century European builders borrowed medieval forms to forge the Gothic Revival style.

Distinctively Siamese in its symmetry and stateliness, the *mondop* is not a functional type, but a ceremonial structural form that can be applied to several different kinds of temple and palace buildings. It is distinguished by its square or cruciform floor plan.

A *mondop* can house a scripture pavilion or bell tower, enshrine a sacred object such as a Buddha footprint or boundary marker, serve as a crematory shrine, or stand as a ceremonial palace pavilion. The form is also abstracted in miniature as the decorative framework around the windows of palace buildings and royal temples.

The Thai form of the *mondop* was probably influenced by the similar Burmese *mondop*, which in turn was based on South Asian models. It differs from the *mandapa* of Khmer and Indian temple construction, which are the entrance chambers on one or more of the four sides of the sanctuary of a *sikhara* or *prang* memorial tower. Whereas these are essentially elements of a larger structure, the Thai *mondop* is a free-standing unit.

The *mondop* form, used since the Sukhothai period, has been applied extensively in royal temples constructed in and around Bangkok since the capital's founding. Prime examples are the Phra Mondop scripture pavilions at Wat Pho and at the Temple of the Emerald Buddha in the Grand Palace, various *mondops* at Thonburi's Wat Arun, and the grand *mondop* housing a Buddha footprint at Saraburi.

4.12 Crematoriums

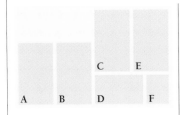

A. *The exceptionally fine architecture of this crematorium at Bangkok's Wat Thepsirin graces the funerals of members of royalty and other eminent persons.*

B. *Mourners pay their last respects at a funeral held at another crematorium at Wat Thepsirin.*

C. *The crematorium at Wat Makutkasat hosts many large Bangkok funerals.*

D. *The crematorium at Thonburi's Wat Prayun is fronted by a pavilion in a simplified mondop form. The temple was founded in 1828 by a patriarch of the Bunnag clan.*

E. *Behind Thonburi's Wat Arun is this classic Rattanakosin crematorium.*

F. *Central-style architecture influenced the design of this crematorium in the northeastern province of Ubon Ratchathani, at Wat Thung Sriwilai.*

Buddhist funerals end with the cremation of the body, a ritual served by the special architecture used for the crematorium. Called a *meru*, its name refers to the Buddhist–Hindu cosmology of Mount Meru, the divine peak symbolising the afterlife. This reference is underscored by the building's structure, which usually takes the form of a *mondop*, a square hall on a three-tiered base with a spired, multi-tiered roof. In this, the *meru* for a commoner is much like its royal counterpart, the *phra merumas* (see 5.5 Royal Funeral Architecture), except that the ordinary version is less elaborately decorated and is a permanent structure, usually built of masonry, unlike the temporary royal pyre made of wood.

The *mondop* hall is used for the ceremonial display of the corpse in a decorated coffin while mourners pay their respects. An anterior room or verandah provides a space for monks to chant prayers. Adjoining the *mondop* is a second, rectangular structure that contains a cremation chamber with a furnace and chimney. The cremation produces a small pile of ashes which relatives place in a memorial urn or scatter over water.

The *meru* is usually built within the temple compound or at the village fringe. *Merus* were not installed in temples within the original Rattanakosin area. King Rama I banned them from the royal district, probably because so soon after the sacking of Ayutthaya, the smell of a burning corpse was inauspicious.

4.13 Northern Temples

A, C & D. Viharn Lai Kham's murals, painted in the 1820s, show the liveliness and naturalism of Lanna style. The exterior is seen in photo C.

B. The multi-tiered roofs of Lanna temples telescope beyond the main roof as in central Siamese architecture, but much further, usually spilling forward over a redented floor plan, with a balustrade guarded by naga figures.

E. A folkish yak guardian figure decorates the top of a post at Phrae's Wat Luang.

F & G. Emblems of Lanna religious architecture are hamsa figures and the Burmese-influenced hti, or sacred parasol, as seen at Lampang's Wat Phra That Lampang Luang. The temple's main Buddha image is housed in a seven-tiered, gilded ku, a chedi-like reliquary unique to Lanna architecture.

H. Some Lanna temple halls feature a fully open or partly enclosed design with roofs that dip very low to block the sun and rain, as in the open portico of this viharn.

I. Nan province's Wat Phumin combines the viharn and ubosot in the same cruciform hall, a gem of Lanna architecture famed for its murals and undulating naga balustrades. Founded in 1596, the temple's present design dates from a late 19th-century renovation.

J. Wat Bun Yeun was built by the lord of Nan in the late 18th century. Its main hall combines the ubosot and viharn under a four-tiered roof.

K. Phrae's key temple is Wat Luang. In the foreground is its old ubosot. The larger chapel, with hamsa apex finials, combines a viharn and ubosot.

Northern Thailand, where the first Tai chiefdoms emerged in the 12th century, retains a distinctive culture and architecture to this day. The most important of the dominions in the north was known as Lanna, meaning 'Land of a Million Rice Fields', a group of kingdoms centred in Chiang Mai that lasted from the 13th to the 18th centuries. The region, which had cultural and political affiliations with principalities in Laos and southern China, was not absorbed into Siam until the 19th century.

Temple halls in the north are smaller and less elaborate than in central Thailand. Wood ornament predominates, sometimes gilded or decorated with glass tiles. In general, the look inside and out is freer, gentler and less regimented. The roof area is larger, sweeping low towards the ground to cover more of the wall. Multi-tiered roofs have lower tiers that telescope much farther, over redented floor plans. Unique to the north are *viharns* built as open pavilions.

Burmese architecture has also had an influence—a legacy of conquest, migration and trade. Much of Lanna was occupied by the Burmese for more than 200 years after 1558. Temples they built there featured characteristic *pyatthat* roofs in three, five, seven or nine tiers of rectangular pyramids, recalling Chinese pagodas. Other Burmese decorative traits were introduced by craftsmen and traders of the Tai ethnic minorities known as the Shan, or Tai Yai in Thailand. The Shan populace is centred in northern Burma, but many groups have travelled and settled along trade routes in north Thailand over the past 1,000 years, ending up in places like Lampang, Phrae and Nan.

4.14 Northeastern Temples

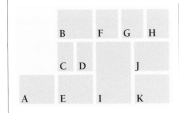

A. *A sim built in 1820 at Wat Klang Khok Kho, founded in 1792 in Kalasin.*

B. *The sim at Wat Sri Than, also known as Wat Ban Nat, in Roi Et, also shown here in photo J.*

C & D. *Wat Photaram in Maha Sarakham has exterior walls decorated with folkish guardian figures in plaster relief and paint.*

E. *Interior murals at Wat Photaram. See photos C and D.*

F. *Intertwining naga figures decorate the gables of the early 20th-century sim of Wat Pho Sri in Khon Kaen, one of Isaan's finest.*

G. *Gable-board paintings on the sim of Sakon Nakhon's Wat Phra That Choengchum Worawihan, from a 1920 restoration. The temple was founded in 1679.*

H. *Isaan folk-style murals at their liveliest are painted on bas-relief designs on the walls of the 1832 sim of Wat Sra Thong, in Khon Kaen.*

I. *The 1888 sim of Roi Et's Wat Rasisalai is notable for its fine proportions and the eave brackets carved like nagas. Built by craftsmen from Vientiane, the chapel shows Laotian influence in both structure and details.*

J. *Gable boards and eave brackets of the sim at Wat Sri Than in Roi Et are carved in exuberant designs.*

K. *Although it stands in Thailand's northern region, Sri Satchanalai in Sukhothai province, the 1844 ordination hall of Wat Had Siao shares the same Laotian characteristics as sims in Isaan.*

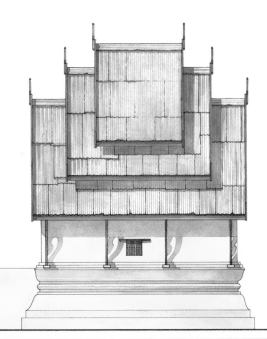

The Buddhist architecture of Isaan, Thailand's populous, multicultural northeast, has been shaped mostly by the ethnic Tai groups who have migrated there since the 17th century, especially from Laos. Temple architecture reflects the Laotian styles that similarly influenced some parts of northern Thailand.

The classic Isaan temple hall is small, simple and built on a high base. Its roof features one or more gabled upper tiers over a hipped lower tier. An ordination hall is locally called a *sim*, a term derived from the word *sema* or *sima*, meaning sacred boundary (as in *bai sema*). The *sim* used to be built as a floating structure called a *sim nam*, now nearly extinct. Since the *sim* was traditionally used only for monastic rites, it was built just large enough to accommodate 21 monks.

Sims built on land can be made of wood or plastered brick, partly enclosed by walls or fully open. A rustic *sim* may simply have gable coverings made from carpentered boards, like on a house, with a floor made of packed earth and a roof of corrugated iron. Temples with masonry walls feature murals painted on the exterior in a folkish style distinctive to Isaan. Laotian-influenced *sim* may have eave brackets that are each carved with a different design rather than the identical pattern seen in the central region. The Isaan *wat* usually also features a sermon hall called a *ho chaek*, and a *sim*-like *viharn*.

Many temples in Isaan have been built in the central style since Bangkok gained control there in the 18th century.

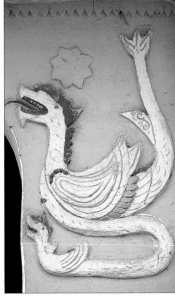

4.15 Southern Temples

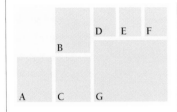

Southern *wats* show a mix of local influences and central style. The region was increasingly integrated with central Siam during the early Rattanakosin years, and King Rama V made many visits to the region. *Ubosots*, *viharns* and other main temple structures built or renovated there during the 19th century often reflect a central influence, including Chinese decoration and motifs prevalent in the capital.

More eclectic local style is often seen in secondary buildings such as monks' quarters. Malay and Sino-Portuguese influence shows up in many features, including colourfully painted motifs, wooden fretwork and hipped roofs, even multi-tiered hipped roofs recalling vernacular timber mosques of Malaysia and Indonesia (see 4.16 Mosques).

One grand example is the abbot's residence at Wat Choltara Singhae in Narathiwat, the Muslim deep south. This *wat* made history in 1909 due to its inclusion of a central-style *viharn*. When Siam was negotiating how much southern territory it would cede to Britain, officials cited the *viharn* as proof of the district's Thai identity, successfully keeping Siam's borders some 25 km further south than Britain first demanded.

4.16 Mosques

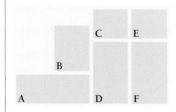

Some 13% of Thailand's populace is Muslim, and there are some 3,000 mosques in the country, yet Thai Islamic architecture has been almost entirely neglected in publishing. The oldest Thai mosques date to the Ayutthaya period. These show local characteristics not seen in the many Muslim sites of worship that have been built more recently in Indian Moghul or Middle Eastern styles.

In Bangkok, Thonburi and Ayutthaya, for example, there are a number of important mosques done in eclectic Rattanakosin style, combining Western, Moorish and Southeast Asian forms. Many have undergone renovations that have erased their original exteriors, but Siamese stylistics show on interior elements such as the minbar, or pulpit, and the mihrab, the decorated niche on the wall facing Mecca. Some of these mosques have long enjoyed royal patronage, a manifestation of centuries-old Thai traditions of religious tolerance and multiculturalism.

Up to 99% of all Thai Muslims are Sunni, and most of them are of ethnic Malay origin. Thailand's non-Malay Muslims are mostly descendants of traders from the Middle East, South Asia and Persia. The Ayutthaya kingdom had an important settlement of Shiites founded in 1595 by the Persian Sheikh Ahmad il Khumi, who became a key advisor to King Song Tham. Descendants of this community founded the Bunnag

family and other important Thai clans. The mosque established by Sheikh Ahmad is shown on page 115.

Islamic architecture in the south, especially in the four deep south provinces where Muslims are a majority, is highlighted by timber mosques with Malay characteristics such as hipped roofs. A renowned example is Narathiwat's Masjid Telok Manok, also known as Taloh Manoh Mosque or Wadi Al-Hussein Mosque, built in 1624 (see images A and B).

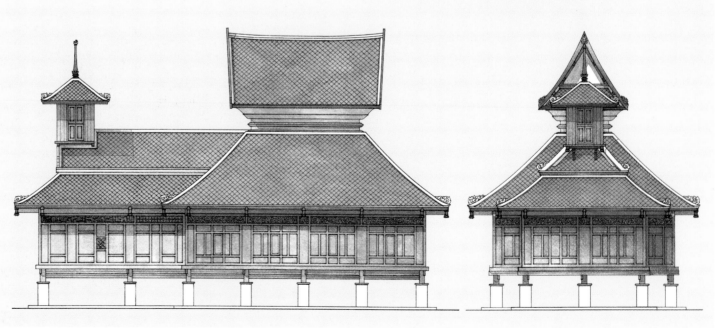

A–E. Bangkok's Chakrapong Mosque, or Wat Tongpu, was founded in 1779, but the existing two-storey cement structure replaced the wooden original in 1966. The carved and gilded wood elements of the old minbar and mihrab hint at what might have been the architectural style of the old building.

F. Dating to the 1620s, Ayutthaya's Takiaayokin Mosque was founded by Sheik Ahmad il Khumi, or Chao Khun Takia, a Shiite from Qom, Persia. The current name of the mosque was granted by King Rama IV.

G & J. Sheik Ahmad's tomb stands on grounds not far from another important grave.

H, I & K. The minbar and mihrab feature gable finials, pediments and other decorations in a Siamese style similar to Buddhist chapels.

4.17 Spirit Houses

Animism is as much a Thai religious practice as Buddhism, with its own sacred architecture—the miniature houses, temples and palaces built as shrines (*san*) for guardian spirits of the land (*phra phum*, a Sanskrit-derived term). Before modern times, these shrines were community structures built for communal benefit—one per village. These days, however, Thais build at least one to guard each house and building, and erect shrines in the forest and near roads, rice fields, ponds and caves. By this count, spirit houses probably outnumber any other type of building in Thailand.

A *san phra phum* is installed when a new building is constructed in order to placate the spirit displaced by the project. It must be far enough from the building to stand outside its shadow, and be installed at a time recommended as propitious by a Brahmin priest or astrologer. A ceremony then takes place inviting the spirit to move in and become the area's guardian. The shrine is populated with figurines of humans, elephants and horses which are meant to act as servants to the spirit, who is represented by a small ceramic or plastic statue. Regular offerings of lit candles, incense, flowers, food and drink ensure that the spirit will protect rather than harm.

The architectural styles of these shrines vary according to the preferences of the site owner, local custom and the type of spirit being venerated. They range from wooden models of the humblest Thai house, to plaster temple halls and palaces with multi-tiered roofs. Bangkok office towers are often mated with modernist spirit houses, designed by architects in materials like cement, stone, metal or glass.

The Grand Palace

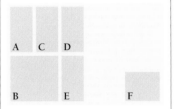

A. The Emerald Buddha is shown here wearing the jewelled cloak which is draped over it for the cool season.

B. King Rama V fashioned a modern image for the Thai monarchy, that of an Asian counterpart equal to the royal houses of Europe. He journeyed there twice, meeting sovereigns throughout the continent and commissioning royal family portraits in the Western aristocratic style. This 1899 painting by the Florentine Edoardo Gelli is now housed in Chakri Throne Hall.

C. Topped by a nine-tiered royal parasol, the Bhadraphitha Coronation Throne in Thaksin Throne Hall is where the king receives the royal regalia.

D. The roof finials of spired throne halls in the Grand Palace are the most formal and elaborate in all of Thai architecture. They are symbols of the king's divine status.

E. Chakri Throne Hall's central chamber hosts the king's receptions of foreign ambassadors, banquets for visiting heads of state and other important ceremonies.

F. Wat Phra Kaew's presence within the Grand Palace underscores the king's role as a protector of Buddhism.

Preceding pages: The seven-tiered spires of Chakri Maha Prasat are the grandest of all roofs in the Grand Palace. King Rama V had the palace building completed in 1882 to celebrate the 100th anniversary of the Chakri dynasty's reign.

In terms of both form and symbolism, Thai architecture's pinnacle is the Grand Palace, centre of the Thai nation, monarchy and main religion of Buddhism. Its traditional function until the end of absolute monarchy in 1932 was to act as the seat of government, the king's principal residence and the centre of royal ceremony.

Its architecture is not just majestic but sacred. The great halls topped with five- or seven-tiered spires are evocations of Mount Meru, the heavenly abode ruled over by the god Indra, to whose status the king's is thereby likened. Pediments, bases and other elements are decorated with emblems of Garuda, vehicle of Narai—the god believed to be reincarnated in the king according to the Khmer-derived Hindu concept of the divine monarch or *devaraja*. The compound includes a royal *wat*, in accordance with another Khmer-influenced concept of the monarch, that of the *dhammaraja*, or moral king, who rules according to the righteous precepts of Buddhism.

When King Rama I established the Grand Palace in 1782, it simultaneously marked Rattanakosin's founding and the official start of the Chakri dynasty's continuing reign. He built it in emulation of the Grand Palace of Ayutthaya—Siam's former capital, destroyed by Burmese raiders just 15 years earlier— aiming to restore the nation's morale and governance.

The Grand Palace is the definitive expression of Thai architectural style, combining Thai, Chinese and Western forms and materials. Indeed, it contains almost the only remaining archetypes of the classical Thai royal palace. Ayutthaya's palaces were ruined, Sukhothai's were built of wood that has long since crumbled away, and most other royal palaces built during the Rattanakosin period were done in Western style (see 8.5 Western-Style Palaces and Mansions).

Renovation and the construction of new buildings have taken place in the Grand Palace since its establishment. Although it ceased to function as the king's main residence early in the 20th century, when King Rama V moved to Dusit Palace, it remains the site of key royal rituals including coronations, cremations and receptions of diplomats.

5.1 The Compound

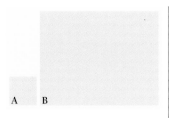

A. *The Prasat Phra Thepbidorn, or Royal Pantheon, enshrines statues of the Chakri dynasty kings. The golden statue in the centre represents King Rama I.*

B. *As highlighted in this rendering, the Central Court contains the royal residences and spired throne halls.*

King Rama I laid out Rattanakosin's Grand Palace in a format similar to the vanquished capital in Ayutthaya. It faces the Chao Phraya River for ease of transportation by royal barge; it contains a royal *wat*; and it stands within an island formed by the digging of a canal, for better defence. Today, the compound covers some 24 hectares or 152 *rai*, and is surrounded by fortified walls topped by six octagonal and three square towers. The walls form an uneven trapezoid with sides ranging from 360 m to 630 m in length, for a circumference of nearly 2 km.

Of the compound's four sections, the most important is the Central Court, containing the royal residences, or *maha monthian*, and the spired throne halls, or *maha prasat*. The Central Court is where the king lived and presided over affairs of state and ceremonies. The heavily walled Inner Court, which includes part of the *maha monthian*, encompasses residences that were strictly reserved for the king's vast royal household, which included royal consorts, young sons, daughters, concubines and many attendants, guards and officials, all of them women. Mostly offices fill the Outer Court, formerly including the Royal Treasury and other civil and military branches of government.

Almost all of the classical Thai architecture in the Grand Palace was erected during the first four reigns of the Chakri dynasty. King Rama V added many western buildings as well as the vast Chakri Throne Hall, a Western-style palace topped by three Siamese spires.

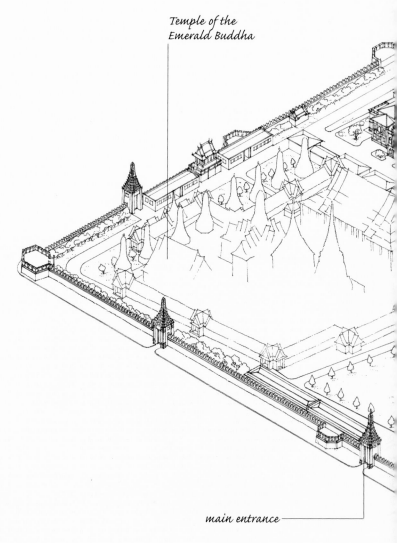

Temple of the Emerald Buddha

main entrance

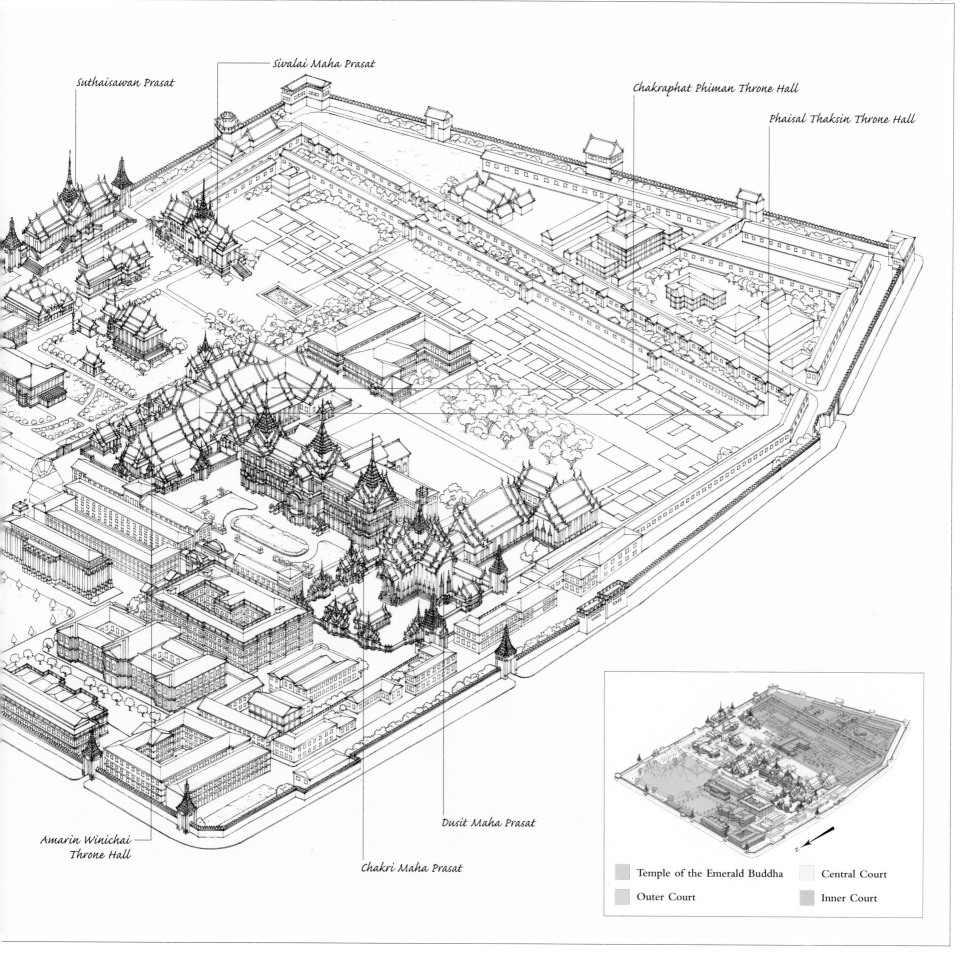

Suthaisawan Prasat

Sivalai Maha Prasat

Chakraphat Phiman Throne Hall

Phaisal Thaksin Throne Hall

Amarin Winichai
Throne Hall

Chakri Maha Prasat

Dusit Maha Prasat

Temple of the Emerald Buddha

Central Court

Outer Court

Inner Court

5.2 Spired Throne Halls – *Prasat* and *Maha Prasat*

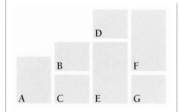

A. *The august central hall of Chakri Maha Prasat hosts the most important state ceremonies.*

B. *Bronze busts of European royalty stand below painted portraits of the Bangkok dynasty kings in Chakri Maha Prasat's Eastern Gallery.*

C. *The reception hall of the East Wing of Chakri Maha Prasat shows King Rama V's embrace of 19ᵗʰ century European aristocratic style.*

D. *Sutthaisawan Prasat, with its five-tiered spire, forms part of the east wall of the Grand Palace. Constructed by King Rama III, it is used by kings for public audiences.*

E. *Exemplar of the* maha prasat *type is Dusit Throne Hall, built by King Rama I.*

F. *Nestled between the mighty Dusit and Chakri throne halls is a diminutive but splendid gem of Rattanakosin style, King Rama IV's open-air disrobing pavilion, Aphornphimok Prasat.*

G. *The gilded* maha prasat *roof form is an ornate, cruciform, gabled structure, topped by a seven-tiered spire decorated with miniature gables and supported by figures of Garuda grasping nagas.*

The most impressive of the Grand Palace buildings are the six spired throne halls, which are designed to glorify the king and to host the most majestic ceremonies. These halls are epitomised by Dusit Maha Prasat (Dusit Throne Hall) and Chakri Maha Prasat (Chakri Throne Hall).

Adhering to Ayutthaya tradition, the spired throne hall has a cruciform floor plan and roof. The multi-layered roof is topped by a spire with a multi-tiered base symbolising Mount Meru. A *prasat* has a five-tiered spire, while a *maha prasat* spire has seven tiers, signifying its higher status (see 6.2 Spired Roof Forms). Situated inside each throne hall directly under the spire is a ceremonial throne, below its own miniature *prasat*-style wooden canopy or a nine-tiered umbrella.

Spired throne halls show Siamese ornament at its most lavish: gilding, glazed ceramic tiles, glass mosaic, and doors and windows decorated with *mondop*-style surrounds. Bases are decorated with *singha* figures, a reference to the king's role as a protector of Buddhism, while royal guardian figures on roof pediments and elsewhere include Narai, Garuda and *nagas*.

As did their Ayutthaya predecessors, each of the Chakri kings through to the Fifth Reign, except King Rama II, built a *prasat* or *maha prasat*. In keeping with his modest tastes, King Rama IV built a small, open pavilion called the Aphornphimok Prasat, used for the rite of changing ceremonial robes before or after royal processions. Despite its size, it is regarded as a perfect expression of Thai architectural form and ornament. A replica was built at Bang Pa-In Palace and was shown at the 1958 World Fair in Brussels.

5.3 Royal Residences – *Maha Monthian*

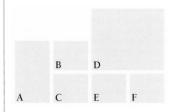

A. *The king officiated at the highest ceremonies from upon the boat-shaped Busabok Mala Throne, at the rear, which now holds a Buddha image, or from the Phuttan Kanchanasinghat Throne, at the front, seen here displaying royal funerary urns. Housed in Amarin Winichai Throne Hall, both gilded structures are decorated with garuda, naga and deva figures.*

B. *A white, prang-spired gate leads to the section of the royal residences standing within the Inner Court.*

C. *The royal palanquin, made of ivory.*

D. *Fronted by a crown-spired triple gate, the* maha monthian *complex houses residential chambers, chapels, courtyards, pavilions and throne halls.*

E. *King Rama II built Sanam Chan Pavilion as a moveable shelter in which to take leisure and oversee construction projects. It stands in a splendid courtyard filled with potted bonsai.*

F. *Interlaced influences: a Khmer prang-spired gate stands next to the Thai-style Ho Phra Sulalai chapel and a gallery entrance with a Chinese-style roof and grille-work done in swastika motifs.*

The royal residence, or *maha monthian*, is a group of structures centred on three interconnected buildings containing bedchambers and throne halls, all encompassed by a courtyard wall. The ceremonial rooms are decorated with 'star ceilings', crystal chandeliers, murals, inlaid marble floors and gilded walls, columns and beams. Inner chambers, not shown here, are more plainly ornamented.

Amarin Winichai Throne Hall is the most ceremonial of the three, with a formal audience hall for celebrations of the king's birthday, the Thai New Year and other holidays, and for receiving foreign ambassadors. The interior houses two important wooden thrones built by King Rama I: the Busabok Mala Throne, shaped like a boat with a spired roof, and another throne beneath a nine-tiered umbrella.

Chakraphat Phiman Throne Hall is the main building in this group, where kings Rama I, Rama II and Rama III resided. The building contains a central audience hall and, to one side, the royal bedchamber, with a merit-making hall on the other side. By tradition, all the kings since Rama III have spent at least one night in this throne hall upon coronation.

Phaisal Thaksin Throne Hall was used by King Rama I for dining and relaxation. Ever since his reign, the hall has hosted coronation ceremonies. It contains the throne in which the new sovereign is crowned, and an octagonal throne for the rite in which the king receives the people's invitation to rule. Also here is an altar for the guardian divinity of the nation, Phra Sayam.

Most of the buildings and courtyards in the *maha monthian* are closed to the public.

5.4 Temple of the Emerald Buddha (Wat Phra Kaew)

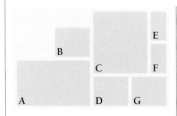

A. Prang *and* chedi *memorial towers, spired halls and dozens of shrines and pavilions surround the temple compound's largest structure, the ordination hall housing the Emerald Buddha.*

B. *Initially built by King Rama IV as a chapel to enshrine the Emerald Buddha, the Prasat Phra Thepbidorn, or Royal Pantheon, now houses statues of the Chakri kings. It is flanked by two gilded, redented* chedis *built by King Rama I.*

C. *The Emerald Buddha is placed in a gilded wooden* busabok *throne with a five-tiered* prasat *roof, amidst a set of standing Buddhas commemorating kings, queens and princesses of the first three reigns. Murals painted on the wall behind the altar depict the cosmology of the* Traiphum, *or The Three Worlds.*

D. *Standing amidst cloisters, pavilions and shrines, the ordination hall housing the Emerald Buddha has a three-tiered roof.*

E. *The bell tower was built by King Rama IV in a* mondop *form.*

F. *Thai-made ceramic tiles of navy, yellow and green decorate the walls of Gandhara Buddha Viharn, a prang-spired shrine built by King Rama IV.*

G. *The temple's upper terrace features a golden* chedi *built by King Rama IV in the style of Ayutthaya's royal temple, Wat Phra Sri Sanphet. Next to it stands the Phra Mondop scripture hall and the Royal Pantheon.*

The royal temple in the Grand Palace is Thailand's most important religious site. It centres on the ordination hall built to enshrine the Emerald Buddha—the Palladium of State, an ancient 66-cm-high jasper Buddha figure named Phra Kaew Morakot. Discovered in 1434 when lightning struck a stucco *chedi* in Chiang Rai, it was held in Lampang, Chiang Mai, Luang Prabang and Vientiane before King Rama I brought it to Thonburi, and later, Rattanakosin. This exalted chapel, where only kings are ordained, features exterior walls covered in Chinese ceramic tiles and gold mosaic, and a base decorated with 112 gilded *garuda* figures.

Among the many structures surrounding the hall are eight ceramic-covered *prangs* standing in a row, each a different colour. Two golden *chedis* flank a cruciform *prang*-spired hall, the Royal Pantheon. There is also a scripture pavilion in the *mondop* form, a number of monuments in the *busabok* form, a crown-spired assembly hall, a royal mausoleum, a belfry and other structures.

Among the abundance of Chinese carved stone statues is one of the Mahayana Buddhist *bodhisattva* Guan Im, revered especially by Chinese worshippers. The largest statues are Siamese, however, done in stucco and ceramic mosaic—the

12 guardian giants from the Ramakian epic that stand at the entrances of cloisters surrounding the entire temple compound. Inside are 178 panels of mural paintings illustrating the Ramakian tales.

Unlike other *wats*, the royal temple does not function as a monastery where monks reside.

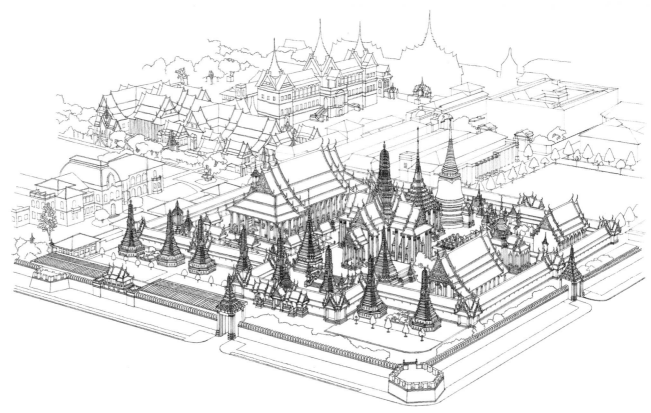

5.5 Royal Funeral Architecture

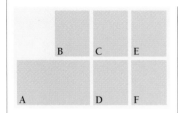

A. *The* phra merumas *built for the 1996 funeral of HRH the Princess Mother, whose son is HM King Bhumibol Adulyadej, stood some 37 m high and was topped by a seven-tiered umbrella of state.*

B. *The* phra merumas *built for the 1985 cremation of Queen Rambhai Barni (1904–1984), wife of King Rama VII.*

C. *A ceremonial gate built for the funeral of Pra-Ong Chao Urupong Ratchasompoj at Suan Misakawan.*

D. *A procession brings the Great Urn to the* phra merumas *for the funeral of King Rama V in 1910.*

E. *For many months preceding a royal cremation, the body is displayed in a ceremonial Great Urn for mourners to pay their respects, as at the 1932 funeral of Prince Lopburi Rames at Bangkok's Ladawan Palace. The prince was the 41ˢᵗ son of King Rama V.*

F. *The cremation is preceded by a triple, counter-clockwise procession around the* phra merumas. *For the funeral of King Rama V in 1910, a manual escalator was built to raise the Great Urn to the platform.*

The funeral of a Thai king is a profoundly solemn and majestic ceremony spread over many months, culminating in the rites of the cremation day. For this occasion—the passing of a reign—a royal crematorium called a *phra merumas* is constructed.

Built of wood and ornamented with paper, fabric, dried flowers and carved wood, the crematorium resembles a throne hall with a multi-tiered, spired roof. Inside, it houses a functional crematorium of metal, in which the actual cremation takes place. The *phra merumas* is a temporary structure that is taken apart after the ceremony and never used again. Each structure is a unique design built for an individual funeral.

The pavilion is erected in front of the Grand Palace in the Royal Field (*sanam luang*), also known as the Royal Cremation Grounds (*thung phra men*). The large space is needed to accommodate the *phra merumas* itself, and other ceremonial pavilions, as well as a long procession and huge throngs of mourners.

In both its name and spired structure, the *phra merumas* symbolises the king's divine status. The cremation represents the monarch's return to the realm of the gods, the sacred Mount Meru, represented by the spire. The momentousness of the rite is underscored by the pavilion's towering height, even when built for other members of the royal family. The *phra merumas* for the funeral of HRH the Princess Mother in 1996 was some 37 m tall, as high as a 10-storey building. The *phra merumas* built for the funeral of King Rama II was 80 m tall, with eight secondary towers at 40 m. A royal crematorium built during the Ayutthaya period reached 102 m.

Temple and Palace Elements

The elements of buildings—roofs, doors and windows, bases and so on—have a greater importance in the Thai system of architecture than in most others. Temple and palace buildings are more readily perceived through their highly distinctive elements than as wholes. The elements call attention to themselves because they are stylised so far beyond functional needs. This stylisation is partly for aesthetic purposes—to create a more complex, dynamic and visually harmonious architectural whole. Stylisation usually has symbolic intent as well, with references to Buddhism and cosmology. It can serve magical purposes, as in the case of carved roof finials that embody guardian figures meant to ward off evil influences.

The elements tell a lot about a building itself, revealing its vintage and regional identity. In contrast, the basic structures of Thai religious architecture do not differ much according to time and place; temple halls have been built as rectangular boxes with gable roofs since the 11th century. Most elements took on their present characteristic forms during the Ayutthaya period, which became the stylistic foundation for Rattanakosin architecture. Surviving examples of temple and palace elements typically date to the late 18th century and after. Earlier elements were lost to war, theft, decay and frequent renovation.

The style of *wats* throughout the central region and beyond was influenced by the architecture of royally sponsored temples in Bangkok. These royal temples feature styles and elements similar to buildings in the Grand Palace and its *wat*. Indeed, many were done by the same architects and artisans. Central-style temples were built in other regions in the 19th century as part of the crown's extension of political influence into places that had been under other sovereignty, such as Isaan and the south. In this way, central architectural style and royal architectural style became the definitive style of Thailand.

Almost all of the elements are rich in symbolism. Guardian figures are embodied in roof finials, eave brackets and courtyard statuary. Buddhist cosmology is expressed in the courtyard layout and the odd-numbered tiers of bases, roof spires and finials on courtyard wall columns. The most sacred elements, to be certain, are Buddha statues.

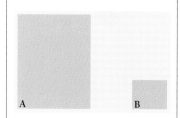

A   B

A. Paintings in the ubosot *of Wat Amphawan Chetiyaram in Samut Songkhram commemorate the life of King Rama II. The murals were painted in the 1990s in a project initiated by HRH Princess Maha Chakri Sirindhorn.*

B. Oval-shaped windows representing a monk's ceremonial fan at the ubosot *of Bangkok's Wat Thong Nophakhun.*

Preceding pages: The spirit of Thai architecture lives in the details—roof forms, finials, columns, bases, courtyard elements and more. Few examples surpass the open-walled viharn *of Wat Phra That Lampang Luang, built in 1476, with its graceful roof and stucco gate.*

6.1 Roof Forms

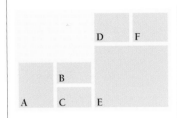

A. *Cruciform roofs are reserved for sacred and royal architecture such as this ceremonial pavilion near Wat Ratchanatdaram on Bangkok's royal avenue, Rajadamnoern Road.*

B & C. *Thonburi's Wat Kalyanamit features classic Rattanakosin roofs. Over the massive viharn, a very tall roof has three tiers and four breaks in each of the two top tiers. The ubosot roof (C) has a Chinese profile and crockery mosaic decoration reflecting the tastes of King Rama III, who built most of the monastery's main structures.*

D. *Wat Boworniwet is another of the dozens of Bangkok temples that King Rama III built or renovated in Chinese styles during the mid-19th century.*

E. *Visual rhythms suggested by multiple tiers, breaks and tile patterns make massive roofs more dynamic, as at the cloisters and ubosot of Wat Suthat in Bangkok.*

F. *The roof of the timber viharn of Chiang Mai's Wat Phan Tao, which was converted from a mid-19th century palace.*

Roofs are the quintessential elements in Thai public architecture, shaping the character of buildings with their elaborate structure and decoration. The use of ornamented multiple tiers is reserved for roofs on temples and palaces as well as public buildings such as government offices, university halls and monuments. Commercial buildings that breach this tradition, as a few hotels have done, are frowned upon.

This is because the tiers, in their decoration, multiple layers and height above the ground, symbolise the importance of the building, which extends from the paramount status of royalty, Buddhism and the Thai nation. The more ornate the roof, the higher the status of the building or of the person who commissioned it. Two or three tiers are most often used, but some royal temples have four.

Multiple roof tiers help to ward off the sun and rain, but their rationale is more aesthetic than functional. Because temple and palace halls are large, their roof areas are massive. To lighten up the roof's appearance, the lowest tier is the largest, with a smaller middle layer and the smallest roof on top. Multiple breaks in each roof lighten it further—a double-tiered roof might have two, three or even four breaks in each tier. The slope increases with each tier, from a gentle 45° gradient on the lowest, to about 60° steep on the highest. In central Thai architecture, the lower tiers telescope a short distance beyond the top roof at the gable ends. On northern temple halls, the tiers project further, often over a redented floor plan that starts narrow at the entrance and grows wider towards the altar.

Further dividing each tier's surface are coloured ceramic tiles in concentric patterns, making it seem as if a single tier has multiple sections. These configurations transform the roof's seeming scale, enlivening the aesthetics of the entire building. Instead of a massive form that visually weighs the building down, the roof becomes a dynamic series of forms that appears to soar. In this way, aesthetics suit the intent of veneration.

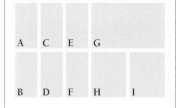

A. The green glass mosaic at Wat Phra Kaew Don Tao in Lampang hints at history. For a few decades in the 15th century, the temple housed the phra kaew morakot, or Emerald Buddha, now enshrined in the Grand Palace. This viharn dates to the 1920s.

B. Roofs over temples in Isaan sometimes recall those seen in northern Thailand thanks to Laotian influence in both regions. This is Nakhorn Phanom's Wat Okat.

C. Even when ornate, Lanna temple roofs exude grace.

D. The roof over the portico of Wat Kalyanamit's viharn has a hipped lower tier.

E. Burmese-influenced temple roofs, as on the mondop of Mae Hong Son's Wat Phra Non, feature a structure of three, five, seven or nine tiers of diminishing size topped by a spire, a roof structure called pyatthat.

F. Filigreed wood or tin enhances the beauty of the Burmese-style pyatthat roofs seen in northern Thailand, often on temples built by Thai Yai, or Shan people. This one tops a mondop at Wat Nantharam in Phayao.

G. Some of the most splendid roofs are seen on royal ceremonial pavilions, such as Sala Samranmukkhamat, built during the reign of King Rama V and now displayed at the National Museum.

H. The curved cloisters of Bangkok's Wat Rachabophit.

I. Laotian-style roofs often feature one or more gabled upper tiers over a hipped lower tier, as on the ho trai of Yasothon's Wat Sra Trainurak, founded by a monk from Vientiane in 1907.

6.2 Spired Roof Forms

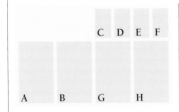

A. Among the spired roofs of the Temple of the Emerald Buddha are the mondop *spire of the Phra Mondop scripture hall (front) and the prang spire of Prasat Phra Thepbidorn, or the Royal Pantheon.*

B. A prang-spired roof tops Bangkok's *Shrine of the City Pillar, or San Lak Muang, across from the Grand Palace. The pillar was erected in 1782 when Rattanakosin was founded. Its current shrine dates from the 1982 bicentennial renovation.*

C. A mondop-spired roof tops the crematorium at Wat Mujalin in Pattani.

D. One of several prang-spired gates in the Grand Palace.

E. The Rattanakosin archetype of the mondop-style spire is the one gracing Dusit Maha Prasat in the Grand Palace.

F. Mongkut *spires top the grand triple gate in front of Amarin Winichai Throne Hall in the Grand Palace. Named Phra Thawan Thewaphiban, the gate was built by King Rama IV, also known as King Mongkut.*

G. One of the most beautiful spired roofs outside the Grand Palace is this mondop *spire over a crematorium at Bangkok's Wat Thepsirin, often patronised by court families.*

H. The roof of Bangkok's Wat Rachanatdaram, also known as Loha Prasat, or Bronze Palace, features 37 mondop spires representing the 37 virtues leading to Buddhist enlightenment.

Spired roofs designate buildings of the highest status, especially royal palace halls. Indeed, the term for a spired roof, *yod prasat*, means 'spire of a palace', or *prasat*. Since the mid-Ayutthaya period, royal palace architecture has called for a cruciform floor plan topped by a spired roof. This reflects Ayutthaya's embrace of the Khmer-Hindu concept of the divine king, or *devaraja*. A roof spire, just like the *chedi* or *prang* tower it resembles, symbolises Mount Meru, the abode of the gods and divine centre of the universe. The cruciform structure signifies the intersection of axes at this centre.

The main type of spire is *mondop*-style, which has multiple tiers of redented squares diminishing in size as they rise towards a thin conical tip. Each tier is decorated with rows of miniature gables. In palace buildings, these have tiny finials such as *hang hong* and *bai raka*, representing *nagas* and *garudas*.

The *mondop*-style features on top of most spired halls in the Grand Palace. Elite *maha prasat* spires have seven-tiered bases over roof tiers decorated with *garuda* figures grasping *nagas*, an icon of Thai royalty. Other less prominent halls, *prasat*, have five-tiered spire bases.

Similar to the *mondop* style is the *mongkut* spire, but instead of square tiers it has round rings like a crown, which is called '*mongkut*' in Thai. *Mongkut* spires often grace buildings constructed by King Rama IV, whose name was Mongkut. A *prasat* roof may instead have a spire like a bullet-shaped *prang*, as seen on Prasat Phra Thepbidorn, or the Royal Pantheon, at the Temple of the Emerald Buddha (see photo A), and above the Shrine of the City Pillar in Bangkok (see photo B).

Prasat spires are also often built on temple halls, *mondops*, crematoriums, gates and spirit houses.

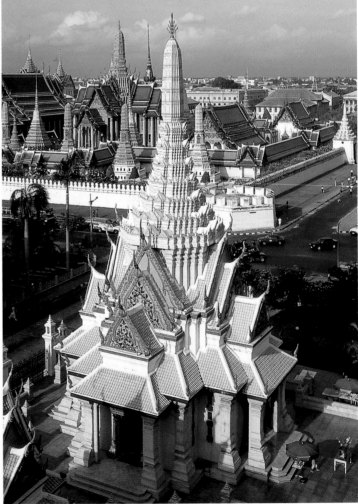

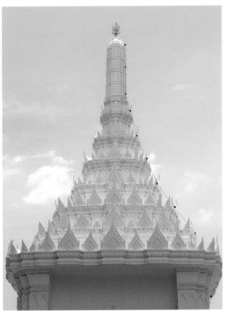

6.3 Roof Finials

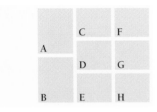

A. Gable-end finials are sometimes believed to represent the mythical struggle of Garuda and Naga. The cho fah at the top evokes Garuda, and the lower finials symbolise Naga.

B. These lower bargeboard finials, or hang hong, are done in a style typical of Rattanakosin architecture, a row of naga heads seen in profile.

C. Hang hong finials on the viharn of Mukdahan's Wat Manophirom have a vegetal kranok design.

D & G. Crocodilian makara appear in northern finials. This ornate lower finial (D) shows the creature disgorging a naga, interlaced with floral and vine motifs at the Burmese-influenced Tai Yai temple of Wat Chiang Yuen in Chiang Mai. Another disgorges a hasadilang, which has a bird's body and elephant's head (G).

E. Naga finials at Bangkok's Wat Tri Thotsathep.

F. The tinkling of metal bells adds to the auspicious and otherworldly atmosphere of a temple compound. These bells decorate the ubosot of Wat Phra Kaew.

H. Makara decorate the mondop sala of Chiang Mai's Wat Ton Kwen.

Every roof edge and apex has stylised attachments that essentially transform the structure into a huge piece of sculpture while hinting at mystical concepts. Most of these are decorations attached to the bargeboard, the long, thin panel on the edge of the roof at the gable ends. While the bargeboard itself protects the roof covering from wind, its decorative structure, called the *lamyong*, embodies guardian figures that protect against bad influences.

Usually covered in glass mosaic or gilding, the *lamyong* is sculpted in an undulating, serpentine *nag sadung* shape evoking the *naga*. Its blade-like projections suggest both *naga* fins and the feathers of *garuda*. Its lower finial is called a *hang hong*, which means 'goose tail', referring to *hongsa*, the Thai name for Hamsa. Although this name may indicate that the finial once was shaped like a *hamsa* figure, it now usually takes the form of a *naga's* head turned up and facing away from the roof, like the *tua ngao* of house bargeboards. The *naga* head may be styled in flame-like *kranok* motifs and may have multiple heads. A roof with multiple breaks or tiers has identical *hang hong* finials at the bottom of each section. Some old temples in Lanna and Isaan have a Laotian-style metal finial in the centre of the roof ridge in the form of a multi-tiered umbrella of state.

Perched at the peak of the *lamyong* is the large curving ornament called a *cho fa*, or 'sky tassle', which resembles the beak of a bird, perhaps representing Garuda. The finial is often erected ceremonially, signifying its importance.

The intriguingly indeterminate shape of the *cho fa*—both bird-like and reptilian—has led to several hypotheses about its symbolism. It may represent Garuda in his mythical struggle with Naga. The other bargeboard decorations help to tell this story: the *bai raka* symbolise both the feathers of Garuda and Naga's fins as the two deities entwine in battle. Another interpretation sees the *cho fa* as a *naga* head, the *lamyong* as its body, and the *hang hong* as additional *naga* heads.

Or the *cho fa* may represent a different bird: the celestial goose Hamsa. Indeed, in some *wats*, especially in the north, the *cho fa* is explicitly carved as Hamsa. Other variant *cho fa* figures are a *deva* divinity or budding lotus.

Whatever their specific symbolism, the *lamyong* figures are all benevolent divinities, suggesting the protective powers of Buddhism and the temple's role in guarding the faith.

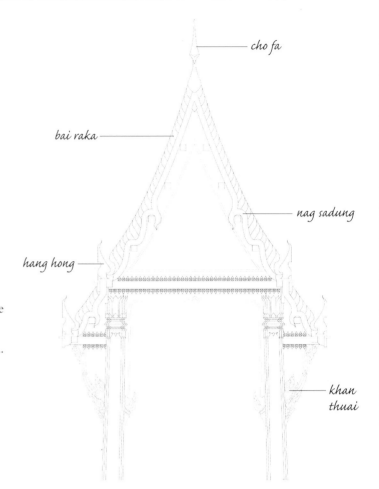

cho fa

bai raka

nag sadung

hang hong

khan thuai

144

A	B	C	D			
				M		O
E	F	G	H			
I	J	K	L	N		P

A. The double trident of metal that tops prangs *and prang-spired roofs is called a nophasun, a Khmer finial that represents the vajra or lightning bolt, favoured weapon of Indra and Siva.*

B. An Isaan-style finial showing a naga with an elephant's trunk at Khon Kaen's Wat Sra Thong.

C & D. A kranok-style lower finial at Wat Pathum, and one in Chinese fashion at Wat Boworniwet, both in Bangkok.

E. A Lanna-style naga lower finial.

F. A Laotian-influenced ridge finial in the form of an umbrella of state, sometimes still seen in Isaan and Lanna, as at Wat Phra That Hariphunchai in Lamphun.

G. A cho fa in the bird-elephant form called a hasadilang above a viharn in Nan.

H. A cho fa in glass mosaic at Wat Chiang Man in Chiang Mai.

I. A lower finial in naga form at Chiang Mai's Wat Phan Tao.

J. A naga at Wat Ton Kwen in Chiang Mai.

K. A 'bird's beak' form called cho fa pak nok, *with wings along the roof ridge of a Lanna temple.*

L. A feisty naga at Wat Phra That Hariphunchai in Lamphun.

M. A cho fah in the hamsa *sacred goose form on a viharn in Phrae. The* hamsa *icon dates from Mon times in Thailand.*

N. A gilded naga lower finial at Bangkok's National Museum.

O. A naga lower finial at Wat Sri Khom Kham in Phayao.

P. A naga lower finial on the Tai Lue viharn of Nan's Wat Nong Daeng.

6.4 Pediments

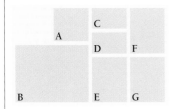

A. Rahu *readies to swallow the sun on the 18th-century* viharn *at Wat Phra Bat Ming Muang in Phrae.*

B. *Designs that emerged during the late Ayutthaya period have shaped temple and palace architecture ever since. This archetypal pediment from the* ho trai *of Ayutthaya's royal Wat Salapun shows Narai on Garuda amid nagas and other figures, with the coiling foliate designs called* kranok karn khot. *Similar pediments decorate many Bangkok palaces as well as temples under royal sponsorship.*

C. *The crockery mosaic pediment of Bangkok's Wat Thepthidaram, built by King Rama III in the 1830s. This Chinese-style temple is celebrated in the verse of Sunthorn Phu, the great Thai poet who served as a monk here.*

D. *A plaster pediment with vegetal and kranok designs that merge to become an abstracted guardian visage on a pavilion at Wat Rachabophit in Bangkok.*

E. *Figures of Narai and Garuda mark the royal affiliation of the* ubosot *of the Temple of the Emerald Buddha. Done here in gilded carved wood with inlaid glass tiles, this pediment also incorporates devas and coiling kranok karn khot motifs. The design has its origins in late Ayutthaya times, and similar pediments decorate many Rattanakosin palace halls and royal temples.*

F. *Chinese-influenced floral motifs done in glass mosaic and carved wood decorate Bangkok's Wat Pho, dating to a renovation during the Third Reign.*

G. *The ubosot of Bangkok's Wat Suthat depicts the Hindu sun god Suriya aboard his chariot.*

The large triangular section at the end of a gable roof, broadly referred to as the pediment, is the most prominent exterior element of a Thai public building. Standing high over the entrance, it inevitably became the most decorated part of palace and temple buildings, where it is called the *naa ban* (corresponding to the *naa chua* of a house). Its degree of embellishment corresponds closely to the building's status in terms of sponsorship and royal affiliation.

In the Ayutthaya and early Rattanakosin periods, the *naa ban* was usually decorated in carved wooden relief that was lacquered and gilded, and sometimes featured glass tiles set into the grooves or applied to the surface. Plaster relief later became popular, usually painted or inlaid with glass tiles, or left bare in the case of humble rural temples. During the reign of King Rama III, plaster relief was often decorated with crockery mosaic made using Chinese ceramics.

Pediment reliefs show figurative designs and abstracted floral motifs of Thai, Chinese, Khmer and sometimes Western origin (see 7.1 Motifs). These *lai thai* motifs serve as a background for pediment guardian figures and as foreground designs on the pediments of secondary structures such as

salas and gates. The pediments of temples under royal sponsorship often centre on the figure of the god Narai astride his vehicle Garuda. This is an emblem of the king, who is regarded as the embodiment of Rama, who is in turn an incarnation of Narai. Sometimes the royal emblem of an individual king is used. Narrative scenes from the Ramakian epic are depicted on the pediments of some important Bangkok temples. Other deities often shown are Indra on his mount, the three-headed elephant Erawan; Brahma on his goose, Hamsa; or Siva on his bull, Nandi. Guardian figures such as Rahu and Kala sometimes appear.

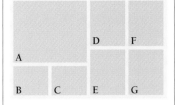

A. Plaster pediments of the ubosot that King Rama VI built in the 1920s at Wat Supat in Ubon Ratchathani mix Khmer, Thai and Western motifs.

B. Perhaps the most beautiful of all pediments done in crockery mosaic, on the ubosot of Thonburi's Wat Kalyanamit.

C. Reliefs on the sim, or ubosot, of Khon Kaen's Wat Sra Thong.

D. Intertwined Lanna and Burmese styles decorate the ubosot of Wat Saen Fang in Chiang Mai.

E. Lanna temples often show central Thai influence, as at Chiang Mai's Wat Pan Pak, where a figure of Erawan and coiling kranok karn khot designs feature.

F. A deva graces an Ayutthaya-era pediment near the old capital.

G. A stack of Lanna-style door arches called sum or sum khong decorates the renowned ho trai of Chiang Mai's Wat Phra Singh.

149

6.5 Eave Brackets

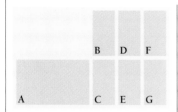

A. Eave brackets carved in kranok designs in Phetchburi.

B–F A variety of Bangkok-area brackets, all showing abstracted naga figures, done in Rattanakosin style.

B. Gilded brackets on the redented columns of the main crematorium at Bangkok's Wat Thepsirin.

C. On a small pavilion, but magnificently painted, at Wat Rachabophit in Bangkok.

D. Brackets on Wat Rakhang's ho trai, a former palace of King Rama I, in Thonburi.

E. A Bangkok pavilion of recent vintage.

F. On a temple hall at Wat Phlapphla Chai in Bangkok's Chinatown.

G. Brackets with naga figures colourfully painted in the Tai Lue way at Wat Tha Fa Tai in the Yom Valley village of Chiang Muan.

Eave brackets (*khan thuai*) are among the most inventively carved wooden elements in Thai temple architecture, and their design is a good index of a building's vintage and stylistic heritage. None were likely used during the Sukhothai period, when roof eaves were supported by peristyles. When these outer rows of columns began to be omitted during mid-Ayutthaya times, brackets took on the structural role of transferring the weight of the roof eaves to the columns or wall.

Late Ayutthaya temple halls were smaller, and their eaves did not need extra structural support. Nevertheless, brackets continued to be used, but as decorative and symbolic elements. They became slender and increasingly stylised. The bracket usually embodied guardian figures such as a *naga*, *hamsa* or *deva* intertwined with floral and cloud motifs. Preferably carved of a single piece of wood, the brackets were also often gilded, and sometimes laced with glass mosaic (see photos D, E and F).

From the 19th century onwards, cement or plaster began to be used in the carving of eave brackets.

Brackets helped the roof to evolve towards its appearance of soaring lightness. When massive outer pilasters and columns were eliminated, they were replaced by these slender limbs. They enhance the temple hall's proportions and composition, echoing in reverse the diagonal lines of the sloping roof, and amplifying the rhythm of the columns, windows and bargeboard finials.

Regional variations are especially interesting. Artisans in northern Thailand and parts of the northeast were pressed to innovate because each bracket was carved differently from the rest, unlike the identical set mandated in central architecture. Figures such as monkeys, demons and *devas* typically appear with arms and legs raised to follow the bracket's triangular shape and suggest the function of holding up the roof.

A B C D
E F G H
I J K L M

A variety of eave brackets showing the figuration common in regional styles, mostly from the north.

A. A praying deva with kranok motifs on a portico bracket at Wat Phra That Lampang Luang in Lampang.

B & C. Tai Lue-style brackets in Nan show a monkey clutching its baby, and a naga with a monkey.

D. Intercoiled nagas at the Lanna-style Wat Phra That Sri Chom Thong in Chom Thong, Chiang Mai.

E. A fantastical monkey-like creature with snake-headed hands and fish-tailed feet on the viharn of Wat Puttha En in Mae Chaem, Chiang Mai.

F–H. Lanna temple roofs are often held up by brackets carved like Hanuman or other monkey figures.

I. A Lanna-style naga bracket.

J. Half-bird, half-human kinnorn figures on brackets at Chiang Mai's Wat Ton Kwen.

K. The snakes on brackets of this Tai Lue temple in Nan are zodiacal references. This serpent is eating a human and a dog.

L. Brackets in a triangular shape called hu chang, or 'elephant's ear', are often used in Lanna architecture. The figure here is a kinnorn.

M. Naga brackets on the Laotian-style ubosot or sim, at Wat Rasisalai in Roi Et, stretch all the way from base to eave.

6.6 Doors and Windows

A. A peacock amid nagas, monkeys and hamsa under a palace spire, all in gilded lacquer and glass mosaic on carved wood at the viharn of Chiang Mai's Wat Phan Tao.

B. A Siamese ban talaeng-style door surround at Ho Phra Monthian Tham scripture pavilion at Wat Phra Kaew.

C. A Lanna door with guardian figures and lai thai motifs in gilded lacquer.

D. Thewada guardian figures above lotus blossoms in Lanna gold-and-lacquer designs on viharn doors at Lampang's Wat Phra That Lampang Luang.

E. Brahma standing on a lotus and Indra on Erawan guard the teak viharn doors at Nan's Wat Boon Yuen. The decorations resemble those on Laotian Buddha images.

F. Foreign mercenaries, sometimes including Westerners, began to feature as portal guardian figures in the 19th century.

G. Among the masterpieces of Siamese decoration are the panels on the ubosot doors of Wat Rachabophit in Bangkok. The door surround is in mondop style.

H. The ubosot door at Chiang Mai's Wat Phra Singh. The circular design under the arch is a dhammachakra or dharma wheel.

I. Colourful stucco designs surround a Lanna door.

J. Gold-on-lacquer designs decorate the door panels of the Royal Pantheon at the Temple of the Emerald Buddha.

K. Lanna and Isaan temple doors and gates are often reached via stairs decorated with naga balustrades, an influence from Khmer architecture. This archival photo shows the chedi at Chiang Mai's Wat Chedi Luang Muang Ma in 1926.

L. The ubosot doors of the Temple of the Emerald Buddha are done in mother-of-pearl inlay with mondop-style surrounds.

In palace and temple architecture, the heightened status of the interior space is suggested by the elaborate decoration of doors (pratoo), windows (naatang) and air vents. These elements feature some of the most beautiful ornament in Thai architecture: plaster or carved wood relief, painted designs, gold-and-lacquer work, glass mosaic and mother-of-pearl inlay. The grandest examples were created by master artists under royal patronage. Doors and windows have plenty of surface area to embellish since they are built larger in palaces and wats than in homes, in proportion to the larger size of the buildings. This also helps shed more light on the objects and rites carried out inside.

Traditionally considered passages between differing realms, doors and windows, especially in palaces and temples, are decorated with special motifs to discourage the entry of evil spirits. Panels are carved or painted with images of guardian demons (thawara baan), or other auspicious figures and designs. Statues of guardian demons, warriors or beasts are placed outside for additional protection.

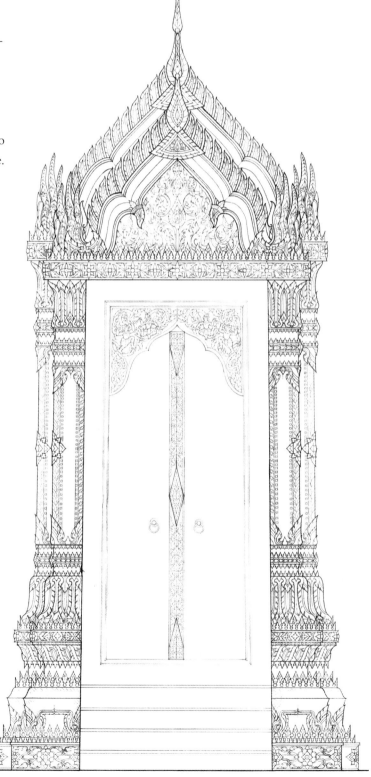

A	B	C	D	
E	F	G	H	
I		J		K

A. A Chinese-influenced surround typical of mid-19ᵗʰ century Rattanakosin architecture decorates this window at Wat Tri Thotsathep in Bangkok.

B. A *sum* arch decorates a window on the viharn of Wat Phan Tao in Chiang Mai.

C. Siamese-style *ban talaeng* gable forms decorate windows at Wat Matchimawat in Songkhla.

D. A window in the Maha Monthian compound of the Grand Palace reflects Chinese influence in both the gold-on-lacquer designs and the floral design of the surrounds.

E. Deva guardian figures on the gilded carved wood window panels of the *ho trai* at Wat Rakhang, a timber structure that was the mansion of King Rama I before he ascended the throne.

F. Window slits formed by brick coursework on the walls of Wat Chai Na in Nakhorn Sri Thammarat.

G. Jataka tales are rendered in animated folkish style in gold leaf on windows at Wat Phra Boromthat in Tak.

H. Ayutthaya-period temple halls often had narrow slits for windows, as illustrated at Wat Na Phra Men in the old capital.

I. Windows in the stuccoed brick base of the famous *ho trai* of Chiang Mai's Wat Phra Singh, built in 1477 and restored in 1867 and the 1920s. Reliefs over the windows show *purnaghata* ever-flowering pots, an ancient Buddhist motif, with praying *thewadas* on the walls.

J. The magnificent stained-glass windows of Wat Benchamabophit's *ubosot* have a neo-Gothic shape under an arch like a viharn gable. Thai motifs and *nagas* are rendered in gilded stucco with glass mosaic.

K. A *kinnorn* figure is stenciled in gold on the red lacquer door at Mae Hong Son's Wat Chong Klang, a 19ᵗʰ-century temple done in Burmese-influenced Shan style. The walls are decorated with some 200 painted glass panels featuring Jataka stories, moral tales from past lives of the Buddha.

6.7 Bases

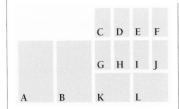

A. At Bangkok's Wat Rachabophit, the base is highlighted by ceramic tiles in five colours designed specially for the temple, which was commissioned by King Rama V in the late 19th century.

B. An inheritance from Khmer architecture is the redented form of many Thai temple and palace bases. Curved mouldings represent lotus buds, forming what is called a thaan bua, or lotus base.

C. The Phra Mondop, Wat Phra Kaew's main scripture pavilion, stands on a high base of marble that contrasts with the glass mosaic of the columns and walls. Leg-like curved mouldings on the lowest layer represent a lion's legs, forming a thaan singh, or lion base, a style reserved for royal and Buddhist architecture.

D. A classic Rattanakosin-style base on the main crematorium at Bangkok's Wat Thepsirin.

E. A base with upturned mouldings on the corners.

F. The base of the chedi at Chiang Mai's Wat Ban Waen is heavily redented and embellished with stucco designs.

G. Triple circular mouldings on the base of a Lanna-style chedi represent the Traiphum, or Three Worlds.

H. The upper curved moulding of this base is done in thaan bua-style, while the lower level is a thaan singh.

I. A base with redented, receding tiers that diminish in height towards the top.

J. The Carrara marble base of the ubosot at Wat Benchamabophit.

K. The base of the golden chedi at Prasat Phra Thepbidorn is supported by beautifully crafted metal Ramakian figures covered in glass mosaic.

L. Sculpture niches stand between buttress-like mouldings on the base of the Mondop of the Reclining Buddha, built by a Burmese artisan in 1937 at Wat Chetawan in Lamphun.

Roofs get more attention in Thai architecture, but bases (*thaan*), too, have interesting aesthetics. Important buildings such as ordination halls, *prang* and *chedi* memorial towers and palace halls are exalted by bases that raise them off the ground, usually in multiple layers that add height, structural complexity and decoration.

Stylised mouldings make massive structures appear taller, lighter and more dynamic. Redentation at the corners creates an impression of structural complexity without actually adding structural elements or reducing structural strength. Using simple rectangular or square layers, bases take on a multi-faceted geometry. Instead of just four sides, bases can have as many as 32. Surface decoration—glass mosaic, gold leaf, paint or patterned relief—adds splendour. Guardian figures such as elephants, *garudas* or *devas* are often applied. Bases are typically made of laterite blocks, stone, brick or cement. Stylised bases are also applied to shrines, door frames and other structures.

The stylisation of bases, plinths and pedestals proliferated during the Ayutthaya period, especially in the design of *chedis* and *prangs*. Mouldings came in two special types, lotus and lion's throne, each with many variations. Lotus mouldings can represent upturned or downturned blossoms, elongated petals and other forms. Lion's throne mouldings, an influence from Persia, China or India, is a stylised representation of a lion's legs and torso. Signifying dignity and nobility, this moulding is generally reserved for use on sacred or royal structures.

Ayutthaya-period assembly and ordination halls were constructed with distinctive bow-shaped bases that call to mind the hull of a ship. Some experts suggest this was a metaphor comparing Buddhism to a vessel of enlightenment.

6.8 Columns

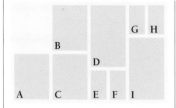

A. Clad in marble, the slender columns of Wat Rachapradit stand on octagonal bases with gilded wood lotus bud capitals in glass mosaic. King Rama IV built this supremely elegant wat as the first temple for the Dhammayutika monastic order that he founded.

B. Capitals at an entrance tower of the 12th-century Khmer sanctuary of Prasat Hin Phimai in Khorat. As Thais displaced the Khmers west of the Mekong River, they started building in stone, adapting Khmer techniques and styles.

C. A tapering shape lightens massive columns. Corners of the plaster columns of the ubosot at Wat Daowadeungsaram in Thonburi are redented once, with a convex curve.

D. Gilded lacquer columns with lotus blossom capitals in an old viharn.

E. Balustrade capitals, called hua med, display the cosmological symbolism of layers seen in chedis and spired roofs. These decorate the base of Wat Arun's main prang in Thonburi.

F. A gilded, redented hua med finial at Wat Rachabophit in Bangkok.

G. Gilded lacquer columns in a classic lai thai stencil pattern.

H. Rustic glass mosaic decorates the lotus petal carvings on the timber columns of Wat Ton Kwen, a mid-19th century Lanna temple in Chiang Mai.

I. Massive timber columns frame the Buddha image at the late 19th-century viharn of Wat Pa Daet in Mae Chaem, Chiang Mai.

The massive, multi-tiered roofs of palace and temple buildings are supported by columns (*sao*) of timber or brick. A large ordination or assembly hall can have as many as eight rows of columns supporting the roof: one or two double interior rows; rows of load-bearing pilasters within both lateral walls; and sometimes an outside row of columns under the eaves of the roof on both lateral sides.

Columns can be round, or, if square, can have single, double or curved redentings. A variety of lotus motifs may decorate the capital—upturned, downturned, elongated or clustered. (This Asian ornament parallels the classical Corinthian order, which uses acanthus leaf designs instead of lotus.) Column bases may also have lotus or lion's throne mouldings similar to the bases of *chedis* and shrines.

Courtyards may also feature free-standing lantern columns (*sao khom duang prathip*) that were used to hold up torches in the days before electricity.

6.9 Interior Space

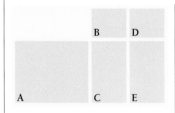

A. Temple interiors became increasingly ornate in the Rattanakosin period. Larger windows shed more light inside. Murals became more detailed, realistic and significant to worshippers as the art reached new heights in the 19th century. Upper walls are painted with rows of celestials revering the Phra Buddha Sihing, the presiding image at Buddhaisawan Chapel, and Thailand's second-most revered Buddha statue.

B. Murals depicting the life of Buddha inspire reverence and contemplation in temple worshippers.

C. An audience hall in the Grand Palace centres dramatically on the elevated throne. A nine-tiered royal umbrella is raised to signify the presence of the king. This image shows the Phuttan Kanchanasinghat Throne in Amarin Winichai Throne Hall.

D. As noon approaches, a monk takes his last meal of the day in the ubosot of Bangkok's Wat Saket. The space in a Buddhist temple hall is no less sacred than in a Christian church, but somewhat less formal.

E. The main Buddha image of a Lanna viharn may be enshrined within a chedi-like enclosure called a ku, rather than placed on an altar. The most magnificent is the gilded, stucco brick ku in Wat Phra That Lampang Luang in Lampang, with seven tiers guarded by naga finials.

Entering a *viharn* or *ubosot* can be a dramatic transition. From the white-walled courtyard, broad and bright, one enters a dim, hushed enclosure. Tall, narrow windows admit enough light to illuminate ornament such as gilded lacquer on columns, mother-of-pearl door panels and polychrome wall murals. At the front is the altar, with more gilded decoration, many candles or lamps, and sacred parasols, all under the gaze of the presiding Buddha image. Except for the lack of seating, it is not unlike the interior of a Christian church: a long, narrow nave between columns, a soaring space under the roof. Hung with chandeliers, the high ceiling is painted in red and decorated with the crystalline floral motifs that form a 'star ceiling', or *dao phedan*. In all, it becomes a kind of palace enshrining the Buddha image—an architectural expression of reverence. It is also a sanctuary, encouraging a state of contemplative tranquillity.

The interior of a palace throne hall, too, is dramatic. The space is dominated by a single, central element; an ornamented throne under a carved wooden canopy or royal parasols with a seat up to 2 m above the ground. The room's other elements are few but stately: decorated walls, chandeliers, ornate doorways and marble floors. The floor plan is square or cruciform, a layout designating a cosmological axis, signifying the king's importance. Traditional palace protocol heightened the sense of grandeur: the king entered and mounted the throne behind a curtain; the audience then entered and prostrated themselves as the veil was lifted to reveal the king seated above them in majesty.

6.10 Ceilings

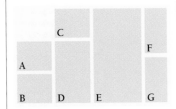

The ceilings of ordination halls and assembly halls have been decorated with lotus motifs since Sukhothai times. Done in paint, gold leaf or carved wood, and sometimes inlaid with glass mosaic, the lotus is usually rendered as a rather crystalline rosette. The motifs are arranged within rectangular or square ceiling panels that are defined by columns and beams. A typical pattern is a group of five, seven or nine flowers, the largest in the centre, with stylised 'bat' designs in the four corners, all against a red background. A chandelier may be hung from the central flower. Although the designs essentially represent flowers, they are called 'star ceilings' (*dao phedan*). Twinkling overhead, they symbolise order in the cosmos brought about by *dhamma*, or Buddhist law.

6.11 Mural Painting

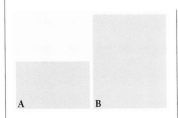

A. *The Mother of the Earth appears and wrings out her hair, releasing all the water ritually poured on the ground each time the Buddha made merit in his hundreds of past lives. This flood tide drowns the army and vanquishes Mara, setting the stage for the Buddha's full enlightenment.*

B. *The ten jatakas most frequently treated in mural painting each illustrate a virtue-abnegation, perseverance, benevolence, and so on.*

Mural paintings enliven the walls of assembly and ordination halls not as decorations but as visual texts designed for spiritual instruction. Much of the Thai public was illiterate before the 20th century, and only clergy could read the ancient scriptural language of Pali, so murals illustrated the teachings of Buddha in a form readily understood and remembered.

The contents, set by convention but open to stylistic innovation, range from iconic to narrative. At the west end of the hall, behind the main Buddha statue facing the entrance, is the iconic depiction of the Thai Buddhist cosmology, the Traiphum: mountains and oceans symbolising layers of the universe and time. Illustrated below is the Realm of Desire, with hellish imagery of errant souls being tortured by demons and beasts. Above, celestials inhabit the intermediate realms of earth.

Murals on the side and entrance walls recount the life of Buddha. The entire east wall at the entrance end depicts the moment when Buddha, meditating under a Bodhi tree, is attacked by an army of demons led by Mara, lord of the Realm of Desires, who aims to interrupt his concentration. The Buddha touches the ground with his right hand to call the earth to witness the merits he has made. (The same gesture is portrayed by most Thai Buddha statuary.)

Murals may also depict any of hundreds of stories called the jatakas, tales of the Buddha's previous incarnations, peopled by Bodhhisatvas, kings, queens, ascetics, Hindu divinities and ordinary folk. Still other murals depict Buddhist folk tales and the Ramakien epic, grandly rendered in 178 panels at the Temple of the Emerald Buddha in the Grand Palace. Add text add text add text add text add text add text.

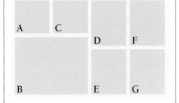

A. *The Royal Ploughing Ceremony as depicted in the ubosot of Wat Phra Kaew.*

B. *Another 'Victory Over Mara'. Murals deteriorate from the bottom due to floods and everyday moisture. Wat murals are vulnerable because the paint was applied to dry walls, not steeped into wet plaster as per the Western al fresco technique. This mural was painted in the mid-1900s at Wat Khongkharam, Ratchburi.*

C. *Devas battling the soldiers of Mara, shown as dark-skinned foreigners on the walls of Wat Phra Kaew's ubosot.*

D. *Celestial adorers face the presiding Buddha at Wat Yai Suwannaram in Phetchburi. Each Brahma, Yaksa, Garuda and other deity is depicted with a unique costume and expression. Painted in the early 18th century, these are considered a peak achievement in Siamese art.*

E. *Characters in Jataka tales are portrayed as everyday Lanna folk in celebrated murals painted in the 1890s at Nan's Wat Phumin. The artist includes such realistic details as the cloth worn by women on their way to market and the tattooed legs of their male companions. Soldiers march in the background.*

F. *An early Rattanakosin mural and painted window panels at Ayutthaya's Wat Choeng Tha.*

G. *Foreigners, both Western and Asian, appear in murals in most temples.*

6.12 Interior Statuary

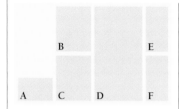

A. Buddha images often line the inside walls of cloisters, a site for worshippers to make merit by offering incense and prayers.

B. Some of Lanna's most revered Buddha images are enshrined at Chiang Mai's Wat Chiang Man, established in 1297 by the city's founder, King Mangrai.

C. The viharn of Phetchburi's Wat Mahathat holds the province's main Buddha images.

D. The axis of the cruciform viharn of Wat Phumin in Nan is occupied by four Buddha images placed back to back, each serenely facing a different cardinal direction. The images are seated in the 'touching the earth' position, invoking the Buddha's moment of enlightenment.

E. The 'touching the earth' mudra portrayed by these Buddha images symbolises the moment so vividly depicted in temple murals, when the Buddha attains enlightenment. As he sits meditating, an evil army led by Mara, the demon of desire, attempts to distract him. The Buddha resists by touching the ground to call the Mother of the Earth to witness his merit. She wrings out her hair, releasing the waters that symbolise the Buddha's accumulation of meritorious deeds over many lifetimes. The waters drown the attacking forces. Thus, the name of this mudra is often translated as 'calling the earth to witness', or instead is called maravijaya, 'subduing Mara'.

F. At Lampang's ancient Wat Phra That Lampang Luang, the main Buddha image, cast in 1563, is housed in a gilded stucco shrine called a ku, sometimes used instead of an altar in Lanna viharn architecture.

An important role of any *wat* is to enshrine Buddha images for veneration. Indeed, the ornate decoration of a *viharn* is intended to create a palace-like setting appropriate for these statues. Thais view them not as works of art but as reminders of Buddhist doctrine or as sacred objects for worship. The main image stands on a pedestal or altar at the end facing the chapel's entrance, amid altars with incense, candles and flowers, often with many secondary Buddha figures. Cloisters, pavilions and shrines may also house these images.

Many of Thailand's most beautiful Buddha images were cast in bronze, but stone, terra cotta, wood and ivory, too, have been sculpted. The monumental statuary of Sukhothai and Ayutthaya are brick or laterite blocks covered with stucco. Thailand's Palladium of State, the Emerald Buddha housed at Wat Phra Kaew, is probably made of green jasper.

The history of the Buddha image in Thailand begins in the Mon Dvaravati period from the 6th to the 11th centuries, and the Khmer Lopburi period from the 7th to the 14th centuries. The Sukhothai era especially is celebrated for its Buddha statuary, graceful and alive with spiritual power. Ayutthaya artisans sculpted crowned, jewelled Buddha images, among other styles.

Buddha figures display gestures called *mudra*. The most prevalent in Thailand is the *bhumisparsa mudra* (touching the earth), which shows the Buddha seated in meditation, one hand touching the ground, on the cusp of attaining enlightenment. Another important *mudra* depicts meditation, a figure seated cross-legged, hands on lap. The 'dispelling fear' *mudra* shows a standing figure with palms held facing forward. Sukhothai sculptors created fluid images of a walking Buddha.

171

6.13 Courtyards

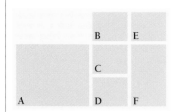

A. *A bird's eye view of Wat Suwannaram in Thonburi shows a courtyard layout typical of urban Rattanakosin monasteries. The inner courtyard around the ubosot is a paved plaza with a formal arrangement of elements such as the chedi, boundary markers and potted plants. A second wall encloses the* sanghawat, *or monks' compound, seen on the right, clustered with* kutis, salas *and other monastic facilities. Behind the ubosot is another courtyard enclosing the viharn (its roof and exterior wall partly visible on the left).*

B. *Paved in brick, the courtyards of Lampang's Wat Phra That Lampang Luang highlight its several very ancient* viharns.

C. *The cloistered courtyard around the viharn of Bangkok's royal Wat Suthat is as formal and beautifully decorated as many within the Grand Palace. The stone pagodas and bronze horses were imported from China in the mid-1900s.*

D. *Wat Suthat's ubosot and boundary markers stand on a high, balustraded platform above this gardened courtyard.*

E. *Monastic chores include the tending of courtyards. At Bangkok's Wat Thepthidaram, courtyard elements include a garden with potted plants, a* mondop *reliquary, a prang and a* sala *enclosed to serve as a kuti.*

F. *A worshipper pays his respects to a Buddha image in the courtyard of central Bangkok's Wat Pathum. Note the sandstone naga statue, modelled after ancient Khmer balustrades, and the* dhammachakra, *or Wheel of the Law, an early Buddhist symbol.*

Temple compounds are enclosed within walls that form layers of courtyards. These grounds assume a greater importance than do the grounds around a Western church, as they are filled with a variety of key religious structures, statuary and ceremonial sites. The inner courtyard, formed by low walls surrounding the *ubosot* is the core. Beyond are *chedis* and *prangs*, scripture pavilions and other shrines for sacred objects, pavilions for meditation and funerals, and plantings such as Bodhi trees, which have sacred significance. A wall often separates the ceremonial courtyard from the courtyard encompassing the monks' quarters.

Circumambulation rites take place around a temple's most sacred structure, whether a *chedi* or *prang* containing an important relic, or a *viharn* housing a revered Buddha image. Often this structure will be enclosed within cloisters. Worshippers gather before dusk and slowly walk around the structure three times clockwise, carrying lit candles, incense and lotus buds in their hands. The three offerings and the triple circumambulation are reminders of the holy Three Gems of Buddist doctrine: *buddha*, *dhamma* and *sangha*, or the Buddha, his teachings and disciples.

Courtyards of major monasteries are typically paved with brick or tiles of terra cotta, stone or terrazzo, often laid out in decorative patterns. More humble temple courtyards are simply covered in earth, sand, pebbles or grass.

Courtyards at the Grand Palace are broad and stately to suit celebrations of the king's birthday and receptions for dignitaries. Lending regal pomp are attractive ceremonial pavilions, elaborate gates and shrines housing royal insignia. Plazas and walkways are paved with decorative tiles, interspersed with formal gardens (see also Chapter 5, The Grand Palace, 6.15 Courtyard Walls and Gates in the Grand Palace, 6.17 Gardens and 6.18 Thai Bonsai and Stone Mountains).

6.14 Courtyard Walls and Gates in Temples

The layers of walls around and inside temple compounds designate the grounds as sacred, and often follow a floor plan adhering to Hindu-Buddhist cosmological concepts, with the *ubosot* representing the hub. Gates, as thresholds between differing spaces, need to protect the area against the entry of evil spirits. When gates are built, rites are performed to invite guardian spirits to take abode and ward off bad influences.

Outer walls are usually 1 m to 3 m high, 30 cm to 80 cm thick, and built of brick covered in plaster. Whitewash is typically used, sometimes with ceramic balustrades, a multi-tiered column capital (*hua med*) and mouldings around the base. Elite temples may have walls of glazed ceramic tiles.

Inner walls that demarcate the ceremonial zone and surround key structures such as the *ubosot*, *chedi* or *prang* are called *kampaeng kaew*, meaning 'jewelled walls'. This is another cosmological reference: the Hindu god Indra lives in a heaven surrounded by walls embedded with seven precious gems. The term thus designates the *ubosot* as a symbol of heaven. The inner walls are low structures about 0.8 m to 1.2 m tall, and can take the form of balustrades, with square, rectangular or cross-shaped openings. Some feature balusters shaped like pilasters of turned wood, or use Chinese glazed stoneware blocks with decorative fretwork.

Outer wall gateways generally take one of three forms according to their tops: gabled, spired or Western-influenced designs such as semi-circular arches. In recent decades, temple builders have tended to install larger gateways to encourage more visitors to enter, often by car.

6.15 Courtyard Walls and Gates in the Grand Palace

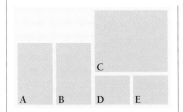

A. *Brahma's face gazes from the prang-spired Dusit Satsada Gate used by ladies of the court to pass from the Inner Court to Wat Phra Kaew in the Grand Palace.*

B. *The prang-spired Wisetchaisri Gate is the king's main entrance to the Outer Court. Here it is viewed through the Western-style Phimanchaisri Gate, used for the king's ceremonial processions when entering or leaving the Central Court and Chakri Maha Prasat.*

C. *The Phra Thawan Thewaphiban Gate leads to the king's residence in Amarin Winichai Throne Hall. Its three spires take the form of a Siamese royal crown, or mongkut, a reference to King Rama IV, known as King Mongkut, who built the gate and wall.*

D. *The wall in front of the ceremonial Dusidaphirom Pavilion is equipped with a high platform for the king to mount his elephant.*

E. *The outer walls of the Grand Palace feature battlements in the same leaf-shaped form as bai sema, or temple boundary markers.*

Walls and gates around buildings in the Grand Palace demarcate grounds of the highest status, from the fortified outer walls, to the decorated walls around the Central Court and the Inner Court zones, where only the king, his children, consorts and attendants were allowed. Gates are so important, often having specific ceremonial designations, that many are individually named.

What are now the outer walls were once the city walls of Bangkok. These plastered brick walls are 3.5 m tall and 2.5 m thick. In addition to fortifications and passageways for soldiers, the walls have cannon towers at junctions. The largest outer gates stand 4.5 m tall and 4 m wide, with ornate roofs.

Courtyard walls in the Central Court and Inner Court, which, like their counterparts in temples are called *kampaeng kaew*, have a variety of highly decorated gateways, many of them spired. Walls around a key palace building may have a triple-spired gateway featuring an especially ornate entrance for the king (see photo C).

Low walls around ceremonial halls and pavilions have special adaptations for royal protocol. For example, a protruding platform called a *kuey* is used to mount a carriage of state, borne by elephant or horse (see photo D), or a hand-carried palanquin. Another platform called a *kuey chai* is used by the king when presiding over ceremonies.

6.16 Courtyard Statuary

A. Wat Phra Kaew's upper terrace is peopled with 14 half-human, half-divine figures including Apsarasingha, who is part lion, part angel.

B. Twelve stucco giants clad in crockery mosaic guard Wat Phra Kaew's cloisters. Each is a Ramakian character with a distinctive costume and decoration. This is Indrajit, whose crown is topped by a bamboo shoot.

C. Old folk-style wooden statuary at Roi Et's Wat Sri Than, noted for its freely carved elements.

D. Western soldiers began to be used as statuary in the 19th century, as at Bangkok's Wat Pho.

E. A Lanna-style tiger at Chiang Mai's Wat Phra That Sri Chom Thong.

F. A sandstone naga figure at Bangkok's Wat Pathum, carved in the style of ancient Khmer naga balustrades.

G. Eight bronze horses were imported from China to guard Wat Suthat's viharn in Bangkok, a reference to Prince Siddhartha's escape from his father's palace on horseback in search of enlightenment.

H. This Chinese stone guardian lion stands in a Bangkok wat.

I. Twelve bronze singha, done in the style of Bayon-era Khmer stone lions, guard Wat Phra Kaew's ubosot. Some, or all of them may have been brought from Cambodia.

J. A rifle-bearing guardian at Wat Phra That Lampang Luang in Lampang.

K. A Lanna-style singha in Chiang Rai.

L. The bronze statue of a holy hermit, or rishi, at Wat Phra Kaew.

M. The Four Heavenly Kings, or Lokpala, guard the four cardinal directions and protect Buddhist law. These were among the stone statuary imported from China during the 19th century for use in temples such as this one at Wat Phra Kaew.

N. A Lanna-style Himaphan figure stands in front of a singha.

Most of the statues in temple courtyards are guardian figures of Hindu or Chinese origin. Rattanakosin-period temples, especially royal *wats* in the capital, are abundantly supplied with carved stone statues imported from China during and after the reign of King Rama III, when they served as ballast in Siam-bound ships. Some were carved in Siam by immigrant Chinese artisans. They typically depict warriors, mandarins and animals, especially lions, as they are the guardians of Buddhist law and temples.

Another sculptural genre embodies a vast menagerie of creatures from the forest of Himaphan, a mythological Hindu-Buddhist paradise in the Himalayas. Many of these appear in the Ramakian tales, and can be seen in mural paintings as well. They include half-lion, half-human beasts such as Norasingh; half-maiden, half-goose creatures known as *kinnaree*; and dozens of others with eclectically mixed traits of elephants, deer, monkeys, birds, fish, *nagas* and other animals. *Yaksas* are the Ramakian ogres depicted in huge statues at Wat Phra Kaew, Wat Pho and Wat Arun.

Figures of Hindu ascetics, or *rishis*, at Wat Pho demonstrate yoga poses. Statues of Thai kings appear at some temples. Buddha statues, however, are less often placed in courtyards without a roof or enclosure of some sort; they are usually enshrined inside *mondops*, pavilions, chapels or cloisters. On the other hand, an ordination hall courtyard may feature a free-standing *dhammachakra*, or Wheel of the Law, a carved stone wheel mounted on a pedestal as a symbol of the 'wheel' of doctrine set in motion when Buddha preached his first sermon.

6.17 Gardens

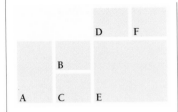

A. *Western-style landscape gardening at a courtyard at Wat Rachabophit, where many shrines house the ashes of King Rama V's royal wives, consorts and descendants.*

B. *Gardens of potted plants decorate the paved courtyards of temples such as Bangkok's Wat Boworniwet.*

C. *A splendid formal garden displays the Thai bonsai, or mai dat, beloved of kings Rama I and Rama II, at Amarin Winichai Throne Hall in the Grand Palace.*

D. *Wat Pho's Chinese-style landscaping is interspersed with khao more, or stone mountains, and stucco figures of hermits demonstrating yoga poses.*

E. *Sivalai Garden is a highlight of the Grand Palace's Inner Court, with its Chinese stone hills, Siamese mai dat, Western-style lawns and Himaphan statuary.*

F. *The plaza of Chakri Maha Prasat is landscaped like a European palace, but with Siamese flourishes such as mai dat.*

Courtyard landscaping shows a distinctively Thai amalgam of influences from Europe, Japan and China. If Chinese and Japanese gardens are a stylised version of nature, Thai temple and palace gardens seem to be a stylised version of these predecessors—not a lush continuum or replica of nature, but something more constructed.

The gardening emphasises the architecture, not the plants. The ground is paved with stone or ceramic tiles or gravel. Plantings are few and formal, with hedges well trimmed, and trees pruned and trained. Most plants stand in ceramic or cement pots, and there are vats of lilies and lotus. The greenery stands free from the buildings. Lacking shade, the many reflective surfaces—the courtyard pavement, the white walls of buildings—amplify sunlight to the point one has to squint.

The grounds are not a sweeping vista to be viewed all at once, but are a bit like a Chinese ink painting or the landscape in a Thai mural—a maze of little vignettes: a flowering tree here, a shrine there, clusters of statuary and the Siamese rendition of bonsai called *mai dat*. Overt Chinese influence is seen in the rock gardens, or *khao more*. The courtyard's formality contrasts with the unplanned sprawl and clutter in the village or city beyond, heightening the sense that this space is sacred, governed by spiritual laws not material ones or the accidents of nature.

Palace landscaping is even more formal than in temples, with more of the pomp and regality of 18th- and 19th-century European style. Lawns with huge Thai bonsai enhance the grandeur of spired throne halls.

Quite informal, however, are the outer grounds of a suburban or rural temple, which tend to feature a big open space or garden (*laan*), useful for events such as temple fairs. The grounds are usually unpaved, with large trees around the perimeter, often including a sacred Bodhi tree.

6.18 Thai Bonsai and Stone Mountains

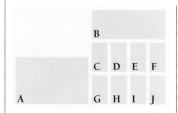

A. *Thonburi's Wat Prayun is home to a huge* khao more *filled with dozens of miniature shrines for the ancestors of donors and their loved ones. At this wat, the monument is enclosed within its own high-walled courtyard, amid a pool filled with turtles.*

B. *A sampling of some of the nine classic* mai dat *shapes.*

C–F. *Courtyard* mai dat *instil a sacred atmosphere at Rattanakosin temples such as Wat Suthat (C, E & F) and lend regal pomp to Chakri Maha Prasat in the Central Court of the Grand Palace (D).*

G. *An ancestral shrine with offerings in the foothills of Wat Prayun's giant* khao more *(see also photo A).*

H & I. *The* khao more *around the* viharn *of Wat Suthat are among this early 19th-century temple's many Chinese-style elements.*

J. *More ancestral abodes at Wat Prayun's* khao more.

Invented in China and perfected in Japan, the art of bonsai was shaped into something new again in Siam. Arriving from China in the Sukhothai period and from Japan during Ayutthaya times, bonsai was first taken up by monks for use in temple gardens. Whereas the Chinese and Japanese intent is to create a miniature replica of a mature tree, the Thais aimed for something pretty, rather like European topiary, emphasising stylised, almost geometric shapes. Explicit artifice, rather than implicit nature, is the aim of *mai dat*, or 'tree bending'. The trunk and branches are drawn into diagrammatic lines, while bunches of leaves are trimmed into small globes. The little pompoms always occur in auspicious numbers of three, five, seven, nine or eleven, and usually on three levels. Larger specimens, which can reach 3 m tall, are planted in the ground.

Nowadays, *mai dat* is practiced widely beyond the temple and palace courtyards where it originated. It is common in suburban gardens and in front of banks and gas stations. But it has had strongly aristocratic associations since the time of King Rama I, who made it his favourite hobby. He planted *mai dat* around the Amarin Winichai Throne Hall and other courtyards in the Grand Palace. King Rama II took up the hobby too, as did many nobles.

Stone mountains, or *khao more*, are formed by piling or cementing rocks together to resemble miniature mountains, a symbol of Mount Meru. They are often interspersed with a pool or small statues. Chinese in origin, *khao more* were built in Wat Pho and other Bangkok temples and palaces constructed during the 19th century.

Temple and Palace Ornament

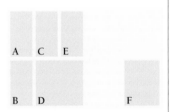

A. C. E.

B. D. F.

A. *Gilding, glass mosaic and a praying* theppanom *decorate the base of a* busabok *altar at Wat Matchimawat in Songkhla.*

B. *A deva in gilded lacquer on wood at Phra Pathom's chedi in Nakhorn Pathom.*

C. *A thewada figure stenciled in gold leaf on red lacquer on a viharn door at Lampang's Wat Suchada, built in the early 19ᵗʰ century.*

D. *Gilded garudas grasping nagas guard the base of Wat Phra Kaew's ubosot. This hall, which houses the nation's most sacred image, the Emerald Buddha, is marked by the most lavish ornament of any temple structure in Thailand.*

E. *A Lanna-style naga in stucco.*

F. *The five-coloured ceramic tiles decorating Bangkok's Wat Rachabophit were designed by a Thai artist and kilned in China.*

The final layer of Thai architecture, its lavish ornamentation, is the layer that is most unique to Thailand. Yet most Thai ornamental crafts and motifs were adopted from other cultures. What makes Thai ornament 'Thai' is its eclecticism, stylisation and floridness. Wood is not just carved into decorative motifs and figures, but carved *and* lacquered *and* gilded *and* inlaid with glass mosaic. Floral designs are pushed to the edge of pure abstraction, typically rendered in myriad pattern of fine detail.

Ornament represents the last layer in Thai architecture in two different senses. In the construction process itself, it is the last step. And in the historical sense—in the evolution of Thai architecture—the forms that were added most recently were forms of ornament. Most of these forms were imported and adapted for local use during the Ayutthaya and early Rattanakosin periods—mother-of-pearl inlay, crockery mosaic and glass mosaic, for example. The origins of many forms of Thai architectural ornament can be traced to China, a legacy of the frequent waves of Chinese influence on Thailand over the past 900 years.

The various types of architectural decoration were included among the ten classic crafts, or *chang sip moo*, that were practiced among guilds based on apprenticeship and inheritance. These guilds, which relied on royal patronage, included drawing, engraving, carving, sculpting, lacquering, masonry and other crafts. Practitioners included members of royalty. King Rama II was a skilled woodcarver, as seen in the splendid door panels he helped to craft for Bangkok's Wat Suthat (see page 190, photo C).

The royal guild system ensured a highly standardised style of architectural decoration within central Siam. Yet official parameters left some room for individual flourish. Greater stylistic variations can be seen in the decoration of regional architecture: the rustic murals of the northeast, the sprightly gold-and-red lacquer designs of the north, and the use of fretted wood ornament rather than carved in the south.

Preceding pages: Crockery mosaic began to lend colour to Siamese palaces and temples in the Ayutthaya era. Artisans chiselled scraps of Chinese dishes and vases into small pieces, laying them into wet stucco to form designs. The ceramic glazes helped the colour to resist fading in the powerful sun. This design decorates a pediment of the Western Porch at Wat Phra Kaew.

7.1 Motifs

A. *Figures like these monkeys are typically shown in a fantastical realm suggested by* lai thai *leaves, vines and flowers. This is a carved wooden gable at the 18ᵗʰ-century Wat Phra Non in Phrae.*

B. Lai thai *motifs can be used in myriad combinations and patterns to suit the specific size, shape and character of the surface being decorated and the materials being used. They can form backgrounds, borders, frames and other design elements. Lai thai motifs were influenced by designs from Khmer, Mon, Indian, Chinese and Western sources.*

The floridness of Thai architecture comes from a vast array of ornamental motifs—traditional designs and figures expressed in wood carving, plaster relief, lacquer painting, mother-of-pearl inlay, mosaic and other decorative arts.

The most prevalent are Thai motifs, a codified set of designs called *lai thai*, which appear to be stylised versions of natural forms such as flames, leaves and flowers. But at least one art historian, Piriya Krairiksh, suggests that Thai artisans created such patterns as the various flame-shaped *kranok* motifs not from nature but from Chinese designs that flooded into Siam in the form of imported ceramics, screens, textiles and other crafts from the 13ᵗʰ to the 15ᵗʰ centuries, a period of extensive bilateral exchange. From these beginnings, *kranok* motifs attained their peak of elaborateness in late-Ayutthaya lacquer-and-gold designs on scripture cabinets and temple doors. Many *lai thai* designs adopted Khmer, Chinese or Western motifs.

Other motifs are drawn from important narratives: episodes in the Life of Buddha and the Jataka tales, as well as the Thai-Hindu Ramakian epic. Figures of Hindu divinities such as Narai, Garuda and *devas* proliferate in temple and palace architecture as guardian figures. There are also local guardian figures such as *chawet*, bearing a sword and book. Thai artisans invented dozens of fantastic creatures to populate the mythical Himalayan forest of Himaphan, or adapted models from Chinese and other foreign sources.

Before *lai thai*, Thais used early Buddhist motifs dating from the aniconic (non-figural) period of the religion's first six centuries before Buddha figures began to be produced. Often used in northern temple decoration, these include such beautiful symbols as the *dhammachakra* wheel, the Buddha footprint, the Bo tree, the *phurnaghata* ever-flowering pot, *chatra* parasols and the sacred goose, Hamsa.

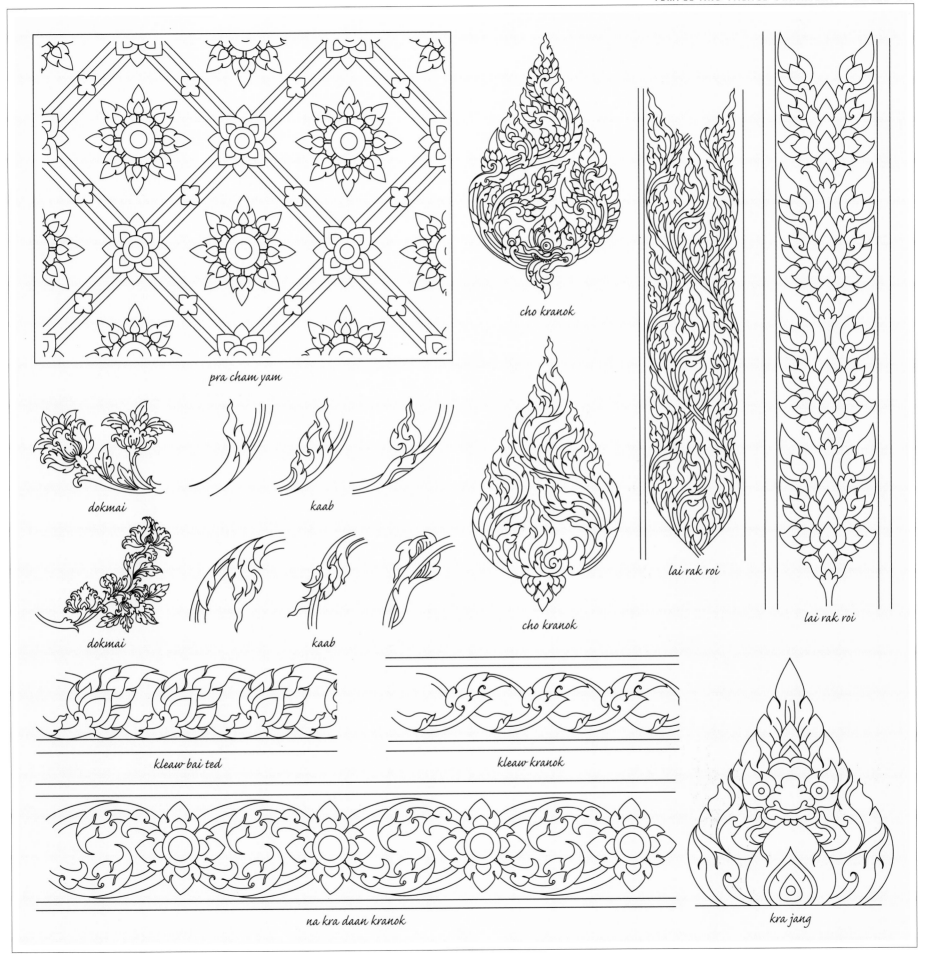

pra cham yam

dokmai

kaab

dokmai

kaab

cho kranok

cho kranok

lai rak roi

lai rak roi

kleaw bai ted

kleaw kranok

na kra daan kranok

kra jang

A		E		H		K	
B		F		I		L	
C	D	G		J		M	N

A. Lai thai *floral motifs become outlines for the gilded reliefs decorating this base at Wat Phra Kaew.*

B. Lai thai *patterns please through their rhythms and delicacy even without the addition of coloured paint or mosaic. Patterns in relief appear to change with the changing light, as on this stucco mondop roof at Wat That Suan Tan in Ubon Ratchathani.*

C. *Wat Suthat's timber doors were carved in this Chinese realistic style by King Rama II. Thai royals and nobles have long taken a deep interest in architectural arts, sometimes as practitioners.*

D. Lai thai *motifs can cover every surface of the temple interior, such as these painted columns at Bangkok's Wat Makut.*

E. *A classic Siamese decoration is this* theppanom *design: a praying* devata *amid* lai thai *flowers arranged in a sinuous, diamond-shaped pattern, as on walls of the Phra Mondop at Wat Phra Kaew.*

F. *The geometric quality of this floral pattern suggests Persian or Middle Eastern origins. The pattern below is a Chinese motif, the* prachae jin *maze design.*

G. *Lanna carved wood often shows the 'floating cloud', or* mek lai *motif, seen here at the bottom, a Chinese-influenced pattern with ancient Indian origins.*

H, I, K & L. *Zodiacal figures such as rabbits, goats, horses and snakes are auspicious emblems which are often used in northern and northeastern decoration.*

J. *A Burmese-style half-bird, half-human* kinnorn *figure on a viharn ceiling at Wat Phra That Lampang Luang in Lampang.*

M. Thewada, *typically with hands clasped in adoration or prayer, are popular guardian figures, as at Wat Phra That Lampang Luang.*

N. *In Hindu mythology, elephants help to hold up the earth. They sometimes feature in architecture as ornaments on bases. Here, one supports the base of a window at Chiang Rai's Wat Phra Singh.*

7.2 Carved Wood

A. Lotus blossom designs carved in robust Lanna style on a pediment at Chiang Mai's Wat Chedi Luang.

B. A kinnorn figure guards the eaves of the Lanna-Burmese-style mondop at Wat Pong Sanuk Tai, Lampang.

C. An eave bracket carved in the lai mek pattern at Chiang Mai's Wat Phan Tao. This version forms the figure of a bird's head (facing right).

D. This hongse figure is another Lanna-Burmese guardian at Lampang's Wat Pong Sanuk Tai.

E. A wall panel at the old palace of the Prince of Lampang, now housed at the Ancient City museum.

F. Carved lotus designs on the kong khiew, or 'eyebrow' arch, over a window at Wat Pan Thao in Chiang Mai.

G. Gilded rice stalk reliefs on the door of Ho Phra Khanthararat at Wat Phra Kaew. The chapel houses a Buddha image used in the Royal Rain-Making Ceremony. The rice design, done in the mid-19ᵗʰ century, has an almost art nouveau look.

H. These panels carved with devas once adorned the door of the great chedi at Wat Phra Sri Sanphet in Ayutthaya's Grand Palace. Dating back to the early 16ᵗʰ century, they are now housed at Chao Sam Phraya National Museum.

I. Timber fretwork carved in a floral design at the Tai Lue temple of Wat Nong Daeng in Nan. Mirrors are a Chinese-style element used to ward off bad influences.

J. Another Lanna kong khiew but with naga heads, at Wat Ton Kwen, Chiang Mai.

K. A kala guardian face on a gable at Wat Rampoeng in Chiang Mai. Kala figures, which show a face devouring itself but with no body, were adopted from Khmer lintels, which in turn were derived from Indian culture.

As the most traditional and important form of ornament in temple and palace architecture, carved wood is used to embellish roof finials, bargeboards, pediments, eave brackets, windows and doors. Interiors feature carved wood decoration on ceilings as well as free-standing elements such as pulpits, altars and statuary. Thai royal regalia are mostly objects of carved wood: thrones, ceremonial barges, carriages and palanquins as well as funeral pavilions and urns. Wood relief is often the foundation on which other decorations are applied: gilding, lacquer, glass mosaic, cinnabar and paint.

The Ayutthaya period was probably the peak of this art form, as suggested by the few antique examples of carved wood that survived the ravages of termites, rot, fire and Burmese invasion. Carved wood design remained on a high level into the early Rattanakosin era. Although Sukhothai–period architecture calls to mind ruins of stone, brick and plaster, there is no doubt that wood decoration was important then too. All that survive, however, are a few carved ceiling ornaments.

Woodcarvers each specialised in a different form: roof finials and ornaments such as cho fa and bai raka; Buddha images and barge prows; seals and emblems; and pattern work on doors and windows.

Before wood was carved, the figure was outlined by a pattern designer. The image was drawn on paper that was then perforated along the perimeter. By shaking a porous sack of chalk dust or charcoal ash over the stencil, the outline was traced onto the wood, which was then carved with any of dozens of types of metal tools.

Northern carved wood decoration is notable for its fluidity and use of animal imagery, while a more formal, stylised mode is seen in central architecture. Wooden fretwork, which is pierced rather than carved, characterises ornament in the south.

7.3 Lacquer Painting

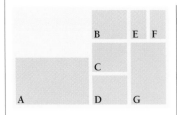

A. Ramakian scenes as depicted on an early 19th-century screen housed at Buddhaisawan Chapel.

B. The Lacquer Pavilion, a scripture pavilion housed at Bangkok's Suan Pakkad palace, is among the greatest achievements in this art. This image shows the interior of the inner pavilion, which was probably crafted in the late 18th or early 19th century. The small trapezoidal chest on the right is typical of scripture cabinets.

C & D. Details from the Jataka tales illustrated in the Lacquer Pavilion include quiet vignettes and scenes featuring the Buddha.

E. Lively Ramakian characters on the Ayutthaya-era doors on the ho trai of Wat Saket in Bangkok.

F. A Chinese-style lacquer design on a door at Phra Wiman Hall in the Front Palace, now part of the National Museum.

G. Another Lacquer Pavilion Jataka scene: the Buddha crossing the river with his disciples to reach the Sala Forest.

Lacquer, overlaid with gold leaf designs, is a striking architectural decoration: regally refined in the central region and rustically expressive in the north. In central architecture, royal craftsmen applied gold leaf on black lacquer to decorate the surfaces of door panels and windows. The same craft was used on decorative screens and the trapezoidal wooden cabinets used for storing Buddhist manuscripts. Classic lacquer designs of the Ayutthaya period depict animals cavorting in the celestial forests of Himaphan. By the early Rattanakosin period, the paintings had became as elaborate as murals and even more refined, usually showing scenes from the Ramakian epic and Buddhist tales. Chinese-style imagery often appeared.

Although lacquer is obtained from the sap of the sumac tree (*Anacardiaceae*), native to northern Thailand and neighbouring Burma, the technique of lacquer painting probably came to Siam from China.

The painstaking central Thai style of the craft, called *lai rot nam*, or 'washed lacquer', starts with four layers of black lacquer applied on a wooden surface such as a door panel, each layer polished with charcoal. The design is drawn on paper, which is then marked with fine perforations and placed on the lacquered surface. Ash or chalk dust is pressed through the holes to transfer the image outlines onto the lacquered panel. Areas to appear in black are brushed with water soluble paint, and gold leaf is then applied to the entire surface. The paint is moistened with water and peeled off to reveal the lacquer background, with foreground figures glittering in gold.

Northern Thai artisans, on the other hand, relied on simple stencils to transfer gold leaf designs onto surfaces that were first painted in red lacquer. They created beautifully expressive graphics of the Buddha, Bo trees, *purnaghata* ever-flowering pots and other imagery.

7.4 Mother-of-Pearl Inlay

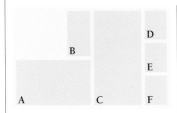

A. Soles of the feet of the Reclining Buddha image at Bangkok's Wat Pho are inlaid with mother-of-pearl designs showing the 108 auspicious signs by which the Buddha is distinguished. Such footprints are symbols of the presence of the historical Buddha. Crafted in the 1830s at King Rama III's behest, each foot is 5 m long.

B. Door panels at Bangkok's Wat Rachabophit depict royal insignia.

C. Detail of the soles of the feet of the Reclining Buddha at Wat Pho (see photo A).

D. A singha design on a ceremonial container showing designs similar to mother-of-pearl ornamentation on temple doors and windows.

E. Another ceremonial container showing a dragon design.

F. Decoration on the door of the mondop at Phra Monthian Tham at Wat Phra Kaew.

Mother-of-pearl inlay (*khruang muk*) is an architectural decoration borrowed from China, but brought to lyrical refinement in Siamese hands during the late Ayutthaya and early Rattanakosin periods. Often used to cover temple door panels and frames, the Thai craft sets a luminescent rose-and-green shell called *muk fai*, or 'shell of fire', in a black-lacquer setting.

Thai inlay uses a different technique and source material than the Chinese original. In the latter, the design is carved onto wood and the area filled in with a shell cut to the same shape. The Thai version instead applied *muk fai* to a flat surface. The shell had to be sanded into slices just 1 mm thin, then cut to the design and glued to the wood. Gaps in the design were filled in with seven layers of lacquer, each taking a week to dry. The finished surface was then sanded and polished. Whereas Chinese mother-of-pearl was made from bivalve shells, the Siamese used a snail-shaped Turban mollusc found in the Gulf of Thailand, a harder material with a more delicate opalescence.

Among Bangkok's most celebrated mother-of-pearl designs are the door panels at Wat Pho, Wat Benchamabophit and Wat Phra Kaew, and the feet of the reclining Buddha at Wat Pho (see photos A and C). Mother-of-pearl inlay was also used in crafting royal trays, betel-nut boxes, furniture and other luxury items.

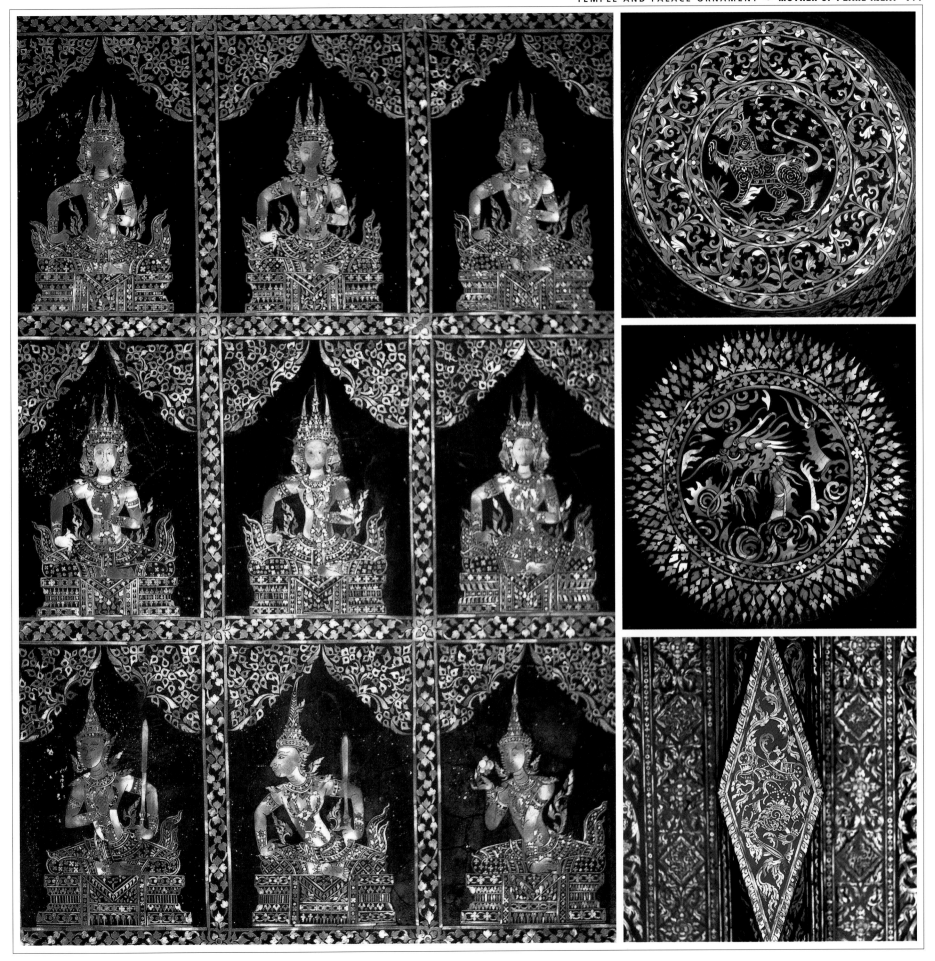

7.5 Glass Mosaic

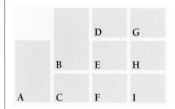

A. Brahma on his vehicle Hamsa amid typical Rattanakosin-style kranok designs on a glittering pediment at the Front Palace, now part of the National Museum in Bangkok.

B. Glass mosaic animates the Ramakian giants supporting the base of the Golden Chedi at Wat Phra Kaew.

C. Erawan, the triple-headed elephant god, on a glass mosaic pediment at Sanamchan Palace in Nakhon Pathom.

D–I. A variety of glass mosaic designs in high Rattanakosin style (D, G, F & I) and in the rustic style of Lanna (E & H).

Temple and palace buildings get their sparkle from colourful mosaic of glass tiles that collects and amplifies whatever light is available—the last rays of dusk, the glow of candles at an altar. In use since the Ayutthaya period, this ornament is believed to be of Indian origin. The squares are about 2 cm by 2 cm, with a reflective backing, and come in characteristically Thai colours that are bright and pure: gold, silver, red, blue, green, yellow and pink. The earliest types were made of very thin glass with a tin plating.

Glass mosaic can be used to cover the entire surface of elements such as roof finials, columns, pediments and courtyard statuary, or can be embedded in the grooves of carved wood as well as stucco reliefs. The tiles are glued in place with lacquer resin combined with banana leaf ash. Alternatively, an adhesive mixture of rubber oil, pitch and lime can be used. By tradition, glass mosaic is not used in residential or commercial architecture.

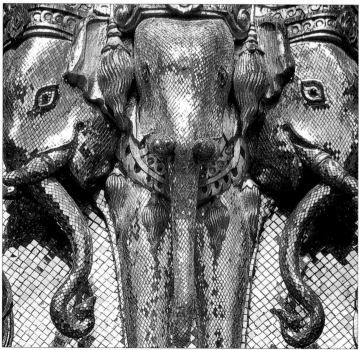

7.6 Crockery Mosaic

A. Five-coloured ceramics designed and kilned especially for Wat Rachabophit.

B. On the wall of Viharn Yod Prang at Wat Phra Kaew.

C. Ramakian giants at Wat Arun in Thonburi.

D. A gate at Wat Phra Kaew.

E–P. A variety of 19th-century mosaics on temple pediments, gates, bases and statuary in Bangkok and Thonburi, mostly at Wat Arun (E, G, J, L, M, O & P) and Wat Phra Kaew (F & I).

Mosaic of glazed ceramic has been used as decoration in central Thai architecture since the late Ayutthaya period, and became especially popular during the reign of King Rama III. This form of ornament may have been borrowed from Persian or Arabic art, since Ayutthaya had many merchants and even government ministers of Middle Eastern origin.

Thai mosaic features porcelain and stoneware ceramics imported from China—usually fragments of dishes and vases that had broken during shipment. During the Third Reign, however, mosaics began to feature fine intact ceramics, often Chinese-made elements which were designed, kilned and exported specifically for Thai architectural use. The ceramic pieces were chiselled into the right size and shape and set into wet stucco—usually in floral designs—on pediments, columns, bases, door and window surrounds, gates, *chedis* and *prangs*.

7.7 Plaster, Stucco and Cement

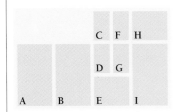

A. *Rattanakosin invocations of Khmer ornamental motifs at such royal temples as Wat Rachathiwat rely mostly on sculpted plaster. This is a chedi built by Prince Naris, with arched niches housing Buddha images brought from Java.*

B. *Plaster is put to expressive use at a Chiang Rai temple being created as an act of pious devotion by neo-traditional painter Chalermchai Kositpitpat. Wat Rong Khun is decorated with elaborated kranok forms to symbolise the extraordinary nature of Buddhist ideals.*

C. *Lanna stucco designs are among the most graceful. Few surpass the thewada image reliefs on the walls of the ho trai at Wat Phra Singh, Chiang Mai.*

D. *Stucco designs on a redented wall.*

E. *Chinese art probably influenced the stucco floral designs on the walls of the 16th-century viharn at Wat Nang Phaya in Sri Satchanalai.*

F. *Sinuous lai thai floral designs bring plaster to life on the 19th-century chedi of Wat Phra That Na Dun in Mahasarakham.*

G. *A door decoration at Wat Luang in Phrae.*

H. *Stucco decorations on the main prang at Wat Mahathat in Lopburi.*

I. *A pediment on a gate at Wat Rachabophit in Bangkok.*

Plaster, shaped into ornamental mouldings and motifs, is the icing on the cake of many Thai buildings. It sometimes even contains cane sugar, an ingredient that gives traditional Thai plaster work its characteristic brilliant whiteness.

Thai builders probably turned to plaster because they wanted to achieve the kind of façade details perfected in Khmer architecture, but unlike their predecessors in Angkor they lacked ample supplies of fine rock such as sandstone for carving. As a result, plaster relief was used instead to decorate various elements, including pediments and the frames of doors and windows. Plaster also helped to strengthen the underlying brick and laterite that were the building blocks of bases, walls and columns. Large statuary, such as the monumental Buddha images in Sukhothai and Ayutthaya, were often built of brick and covered with plaster.

Plaster ornament was sculpted by hand, or else formed in a mould. Thais made plaster by crushing limestone or shells, heating this material in a kiln, and mixing it with sand, oil from *tong tung* wood and sugar cane juice, sometimes using plant fibres such as rice straw or reeds as a binder.

Plaster relief often displaced wood decoration during the reign of King Rama III, the better to render the crockery mosaic decoration which was then in vogue. In the 20th century, the scarcity and high cost of quality wood led to the wider use of stucco and cement relief. Reinforced concrete construction, a Western technique, was introduced in the 19th century.

7.8 Ceramic Tiles

A & B. Ceramic balustrades around the chedi of Thonburi's Wat Prayun, built in the 1830s.

C. Ceramic blocks decorate the gates of Bangkok's Wat Pho.

D. Rattanakosin architects took full advantage of tiles in coloured glazes to create dynamic roof designs, as at Wat Suthat.

E. Ceramic tiles show subtle variations in colour that soften the look of a roof surface.

F. Unglazed tiles quickly acquire an appealing patina of age.

G. Brightly coloured roof tiles are exclusive to royal, religious and national architecture.

H. Chinese roof tiles, with their round ridges, have appeared on the roofs of Thai temples and palaces since early Rattanakosin times.

I. A ceramic roof at Wat Phra Non in Chiang Saen.

J. Moss glazes a ceramic roof covering.

K. The ridges of Chinese-style tiles lend strong vertical lines to a roof slope.

The colour of temple and palace roofs comes from ceramics—glazed earthenware tiles in orange, yellow, blue, green and red. Terra cotta tiles have been used since the Sukhothai period. During the Rattanakosin-period reign of King Rama III, coloured glazes were added, borrowing from Chinese practice. Ceramics have also been used in floor tiles, roof finials and other elements.

Besides earthenware tiles, which are fired at low temperatures, the Siamese also made high-fired stoneware ceramics in the hundreds of kilns of Sukhothai and its satellite kingdom of Sri Satchanalai (or Sawankhalok) by the 13th century. Ceramacists from China are known to have come to Sukhothai, but some experts have suggested that stoneware production arose independently in Thailand as early as the 10th century. By the 14th century, Sukhothai trailed only China as the world's largest exporter of stoneware plates. Also produced were architectural components for local use, including such roof finials as *naga* figures, done in a white glaze or white with a black underglaze.

Chinese glazed ceramic elements, such as ventilation grilles, have been used widely since the mid-19th century or earlier in temple and palace courtyard walls. Roof tiles with Chinese contours supplemented the variety of traditional Thai tile shapes, including squares, diamonds, 'fish scales' and others.

Porcelain, a glass-like ceramic fired at very high temperatures from fine clay not available in Thailand, was never made locally. However, some imported Chinese porcelain was used in crockery mosaic.

European influence brought tiles of terrazzo into use in the 19th century, especially for floors and courtyard pavements in temples and palaces. These durable tiles were produced using cement, sand and crushed marble or other stone. They came into wider residential and commercial use in the 20th century, when mineral pigments were often added to give them brighter colours and enhance decorative patterns.

7.9 Colour

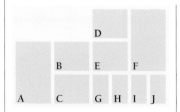

A. *Bangkok's most colourful temple is Wat Rachabophit, clad in five-colour tiles designed especially for it.*

B. *A courtyard pavilion at Wat Boworniwet in Bangkok*

C. *Temples in the south and northeast sometimes take a bold approach to colour.*

D. *More Rattanakosin roof colours at Wat Rachapobhit.*

E. *Lanna's sprightly, folkish sensibilities show in the colours of a pediment at Wat Mae Kham in Chiang Saen.*

F. *This warm hue of green is seen on a few pediments.*

G. *A kuti window at Wat Arun in Thonburi.*

H. *Yellow often appears in Isaan's folk-style sim decorations, as at Wat Photharam in Maha Sarakham.*

I. *An unmistakably red door panel at Wat Phra That Cho Hae in Phrae.*

J. *Bright colour lasts longest in the form of glazed ceramics.*

The use of colour in traditional Thai architecture is almost exclusive to religious and royal buildings. While unpainted wood houses blend into the landscape, temples glitter with colour. Whitewashed plaster walls set off a rainbow of hues on roofs, columns and pediments, all created by the use of gilding, mosaic, ceramics and paint.

Intermediate colours tend not to be used. Thai colour usually comes in seven pure, gem-like hues representing the days of the week: red for Sunday, yellow for Monday, pink for Tuesday, green for Wednesday, orange for Thursday, sky-blue for Friday and violet for Saturday. Glass mosaics in temples and palaces sometimes use all seven colours. (A homeowner may paint the spirit house on his property in the colour corresponding to his own birthday.)

The largest field of colour on the temple's exterior is often the roof covering of glazed ceramic tiles, typically laid in a two-tone pattern with a large rectangular area in the centre, surrounded by a border in a contrasting colour (see photo D). The most common pairings are navy blue bordered by orange, or green amid yellow. This design gives the roof's large plane a lighter and more dynamic configuration.

Interiors are filled with colour in decorative trim. Red is extensively used on ceilings, and often on columns and beams. Gold, associated with good fortune, appears in gold leaf or golden paint, which is especially distinctive when contrasted with black lacquer or cinnabar.

Traditional paint got its colour from such natural materials as ground red stone, wood oil for yellow, copper stain for green, seashell for white and soot for black. The use of colour intensified in the 19th century as growing trade brought foreign supplies of mineral pigments and other paint ingredients to Siam.

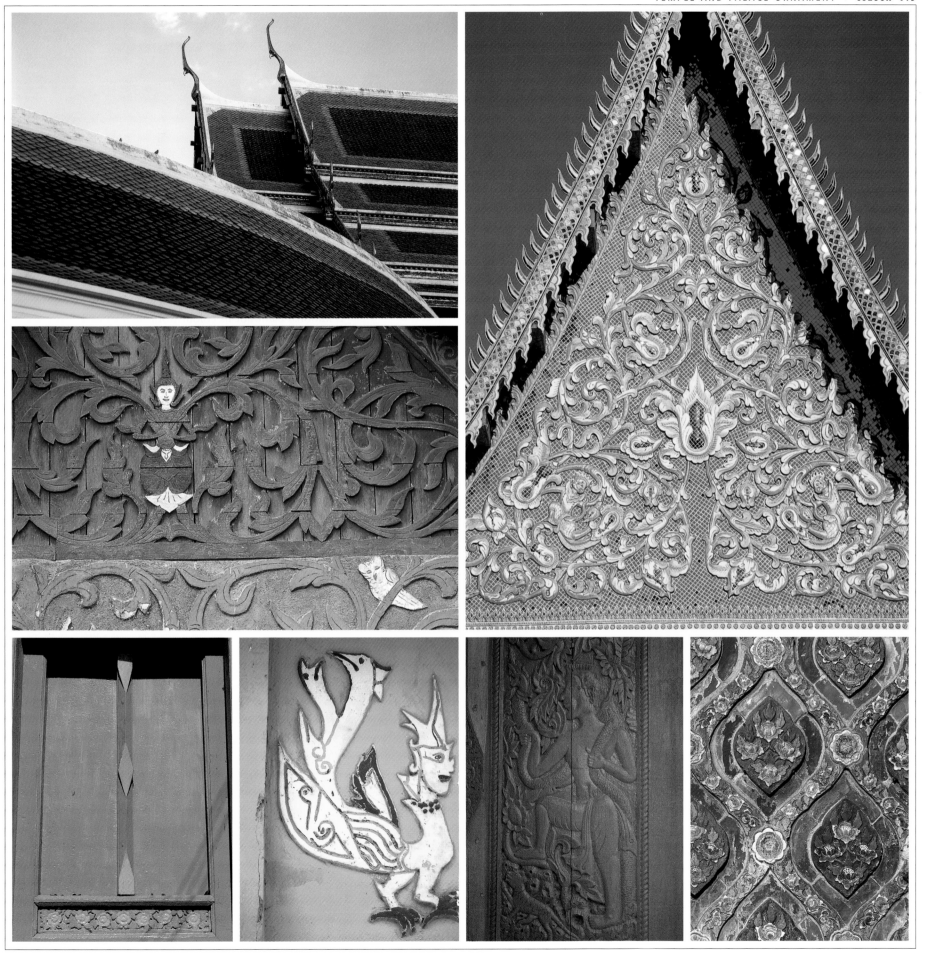

7.10 Stone and Brick

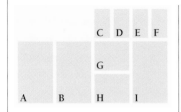

Brick is the chief building material in temple and palace architecture—the backbone of walls, columns and bases. The Ayutthaya kingdom, with its large temple compounds centred on brick *chedis* and *prangs*, was the peak of Siamese brick construction, but the material has been used in Thailand since Dvaravati times. Thai brick sizes have varied somewhat over the centuries, but mostly follow basic Roman Brick proportions. In Ayutthaya times, these bricks measured about 5 cm by 15 cm by 30 cm. Brick was usually covered with plaster sculpted into mouldings or decorative motifs.

The earliest bricks were made from rich clay dredged from rivers and mixed with rice husks and water. The materials were trampled on by foot for a few hours and poured into wooden moulds. After about seven hours spent drying in the mould, they were removed and dried on the ground for a few days, then baked in an open fire for a full day and night. Later,

kilns were used; bricks were baked for about two weeks in a low-temperature fire fuelled by rice husks.

Stone has played a rather limited role in Thai architecture, its use being structural rather than decorative in most cases. The stone available for use in Sukhothai- and Ayutthaya-period architecture was mainly laterite, a clay-like reddish soil formed from decomposed rock, which can be excavated and carved into blocks that harden when exposed to air. These blocks were used for foundations, bases, columns and walls, but were too crumbly to be finely carved. Decoration had to be applied using stucco.

Stone has long been used for elements such as boundary markers and statuary. Engraved slate panels once decorated Sukhothai temples. Booming trade during the 19th century brought Chinese granite and European marble to Thailand for use as courtyard pavement stones, columns, bases and decorative coverings.

Immigrant and Foreign-Influenced Architecture

A C E

B   D   F

A. *Wooden fretwork on the eaves and porches of Aphisek Dusit Throne Hall combines art nouveau floral designs with Moorish geometry. It was completed in 1904 at Dusit Palace.*

B. *Vimanmek Throne Hall, the world's largest teak mansion, was designed for King Rama V by his brother Prince Naris in 1901. An airy and spacious alternative to the Grand Palace, it became the King's primary residence.*

C. *King Rama VI had an English architect design Manangkhasila House in the Tudor style.*

E. *The interior staircase of the smaller building at Bang Khun Phrom Palace reflects the German art nouveau style, or Jugendstil. It was designed in 1913 by architect Karl Döhring.*

E. *A verandah at Aphisek Dusit Throne Hall.*

F. *The Mekhalaruchi Pavilion at Phayathai Palace was built in 1920 as a study for King Rama VI. A teak structure in an eclectic, late 19th-century style, it was designed by Mario Tamagno, an Italian architect.*

Preceding pages: Western style became an official Thai style during the mid-19th century as Continental-style palaces asserted the Chakri dynasty's modernity and status vis-a-vis European royalty. A prime example is the neo-Baroque main building of Bang Khun Phrom Palace, designed by the Italian architect Mario Tamagno for Prince Paribatra Sukhumbandhu in 1906. It is now open to the public as the Bank of Thailand Museum.

Foreign influence shaped Thai architecture from its beginnings. The deepest layers of Thai architecture—basic structures such as temple layouts, memorial towers and *mondops*—were formed during the Sukhothai period from Indian, Ceylonese, Mon, Khmer and Burmese antecedents. In the Ayutthaya and Rattanakosin periods, the main foreign influences were Western and Chinese, growing especially strong during the 19th century.

When the first Tai kingdoms emerged in Chiang Mai and Sukhothai in the 12th century and after, there were already local settlements of Han traders, craftsmen and officials. Chinese potters helped Sukhothai to establish its famous ceramics kilns. As Thais displaced Khmer dominions in the region after the 12th century, China became an important cultural influence; there were extensive diplomatic exchanges with the Yuan and early Ming dynasties during the 13th to the 15th centuries. From that period onwards, trade brought Chinese ceramics, textiles and other arts into the country, influencing Thailand's repertoire of ornamental designs (see 7.1 Motifs). Thai artisans adopted Chinese decorations such as lacquer painting and mother-of-pearl inlay.

Besides the external Chinese influence on Thai architecture, Chinese immigrants built their own religious and residential architecture in Thailand. By far the most important example of this is the Chinese-style shophouse, which has become the architectural setting for Thailand's extraordinarily vibrant culture of small enterprise.

Much of the best Western-influenced Thai architecture was built under royal commission. King Rama IV and his successors helped to domesticate European architecture, making Western style a part of official Thai style in the many royal and princely palaces that they built. These palaces have been extensively photographed and published, thus shaping Thai tastes right up to the present.

Modern architecture is another foreign influence, one that has not often been successfully integrated into a Thai context. Since the 1990s, however, architects have made progress at deploying local forms in contemporary buildings, as illustrated in Chapter 9, Thai Architectural Forms Today.

8.1 Chinese Influence

A. *The Gulf of Thailand port of Songkhla was a major entrepôt for trade between China and Southeast Asia, a history reflected in the old town's collection of row houses and shophouses, some dating back to the 18ᵗʰ century.*

B. *The Chinese-influenced styles beloved of King Rama III can be seen on dozens of Rattanakosin temples, including Wat Rajaoros in Thonburi, where he completed a major renovation in 1831.*

C. *The roof, windows and courtyard pagodas are Chinese-influenced elements at Songkhla's Wat Machimawat.*

D & G. *Ornamental mosaic made from Chinese ceramics is used throughout the Grand Palace and Wat Phra Kaew.*

E & H. *Temple roofs often use Chinese elements such as ridged tiles and ceramic finials.*

F. *Ceramic decorations often mix Chinese and Thai styles. Balustrades at the ubosot of Wat Phra Kaew feature ceramic tiles with Chinese-style floral paintings between blue tiles in lai thai motifs.*

I. *A pediment in a Chinese-influenced floral design at the Grand Palace.*

J. *At Wat Rachabophit, the decorative ceramics were kilned in China, but use Thai motifs in florid colours.*

Chinese culture has had a strong and recurrent influence on Thailand's architecture from the beginnings of Thai history thanks to trade, diplomatic exchange and immigration. It is easily seen in the ornament of religious and royal architecture: lacquer painting, mother-of-pearl inlay and decorative motifs. It is also obvious in elements such as temple and palace roofs built in Chinese style, and in courtyard elements such as Thai bonsai and stone mountains. Chinese-style imagery appears in many Thai murals, and the use of the colour red to decorate temple interiors is probably a result of Chinese influence.

Chinese influence reached a peak during the Second, Third and Fourth Reigns of the Rattanakosin period. Sinicisation was especially strong during the reign of King Rama III, when some 200,000 Chinese migrants, including many artisans and construction workers, came to Siam. About one in four of the 74 monasteries built or renovated during that reign featured main buildings with Chinese-style decoration. Chinese pagodas and guardian statues were imported for courtyard use. Official royal style incorporated Chinese influences, prominent in many palaces. During the Fourth Reign, many Chinese artisans were given ranks of honour.

About 10% of Thailand's population can trace its ancestry to China, mostly to immigrants who arrived over the past 200 years. These immigrants built traditional Chinese structures throughout Thailand: shophouses, courtyard houses, temples and shrines. However, Chinese architecture was present in Siam before the Rattanakosin period. Ayutthaya, which relied heavily on Chinese shipbuilders, sailors and traders to conduct its extensive commerce with China, had three Chinese districts. Chinese-style buildings in Ayutthaya included the Phra Kaew Pavilion, an octagonal wooden repository for the safe keeping of royal treasures. Palaces built by King Taksin, the half-Chinese founder of the Thonburi kingdom, also adopted Chinese structures and decoration.

8.2 Chinese Shophouses

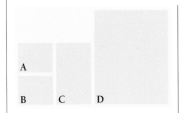

A & B. The handsome aesthetics of the traditional shophouse fell into widespread neglect in Thailand from the 1970s through to the 1990s. Owners replaced traditional façades with ungainly 'modern' elements and cluttered them with signage or simply tore them down. More recently, entrepreneurs have found that it takes little but fresh paint to bring these architectural gems back to life.

C. Muslim traders in Bangkok's Samphan Thawong district—said to be the world's largest Chinatown—probably in the early 20th century. The surrounding Yaowarat area is still a district of thriving shophouse businesses. The neighbourhood was established when Chinese traders were relocated there in the 18th century from the area where the Grand Palace was to be built.

D. Bangkok, like other Thai cities, is still essentially a grid of shophouses. This view of Charoen Krung Road during the 1920s shows many buildings that still stand today, some still vending the same rice, handwoven baskets and other basic goods that were sold there in the early 20th century. Others have become antique shops, day spas and restaurants.

The basic 'building block' of urban Thailand, the type of structure that gives cities and towns their layout and look, is the venerable Chinese shophouse—a hybrid Eastern-Western form brought by immigrants mostly from the coastal provinces of southern China from the mid-19th to the mid-20th centuries. Thanks to its adaptability in terms of function, style and configuration, the Chinese-style shophouse is one traditional genre that is still being built.

The classic shophouse is built in a row of two- or three-storey masonry units with shared walls. The front wall of the ground floor is often made of louvred doors that open the interior to the street for use as a retail shop or wholesale business, while the upper level is a residence for the owner's family. A shophouse can serve as a warehouse, or as a service area for a restaurant, barbershop or similar business. Or it can be used solely as a residence, turning the ground floor's front room into a family room open to breezes from the street.

Laid out as a narrow rectangle, the street frontage measures just 3 m to 5 m wide, but the house extends as far back as 20 m. An interior courtyard or airwell provides ventilation, since the shared, load-bearing side walls lack windows. The ground floor shop is furnished with an ancestral altar along the back wall facing the entrance. Rooms upstairs can be subdivided with walls to provide rental units. Ceilings often feature exposed timber joists under wooden floorboards.

Decoration is focused on the front façade, especially on the upper storeys. This is a legacy of a taste in southern China during the 19th century for plaster foliate designs, pilasters, fanlights and other elements of European styles like neoclassical, Baroque and Italianate.

8.3 Sino-Portuguese Style

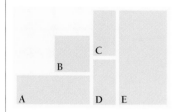

A. Sino-Portuguese shophouses built in Phuket in the late 19ᵗʰ century feature the Singaporean innovation of the covered walkway.

B. One of southern Thailand's architectural monuments is the mansion of the governor of Songkhla, built in 1878 and today home to a museum.

C. European-influenced masonry and plaster mouldings are hallmarks of Sino-Portuguese style.

D & E. Townhouse interiors featured relatively luxurious decorations such as carved and lacquered wood, and floors tiled in stone, ceramic or terrazzo, reflecting the affluence of merchant families.

Many of Thailand's most distinctive shophouses and townhouses are built in the Sino-Portuguese style that originated in Melaka and spread throughout the Melaka Straits. The hybrid originated in the 16ᵗʰ century when Portuguese traders and colonial officials introduced the European row house structure there, which was then embellished by the Chinese workers who built them. Later, the Dutch and British succeeded the Portuguese as colonists in the Straits, adding their ingredients to the mix, particularly in places like Penang and Singapore. It reached Siam in southern port towns, especially Phuket, which traded heavily with Penang.

A typical Sino-Portuguese townhouse features a ground-floor shop, with a living space for the family on the second floor, similar to the Chinese shophouse. The upper storey projects over the lower floor to form a covered arcade, protecting it against the sun and rain. This is the so-called 'Five-Foot Way', an urban planning innovation mandated in colonial Singapore in 1822 by Sir Thomas Stamford Raffles to provide a pedestrian thoroughfare adapted to the climate.

The floor plan is narrow and deep, with a width of perhaps just 5 m to 7 m fronting the street, but extending several times this distance behind. Chinese influence is seen in decorative details such as frescoes and carved wooden decoration, often in auspicious motifs including clouds, flowers and swastikas. The colourfully painted façade is further layered with European features—Greco-Roman columns and arches, or gingerbread wooden fretwork with Victorian origins.

The style is also embodied in some courtyard houses and other free-standing structures, most grandly in the 1878 mansion of the governor of Songkhla with its Chinese-style central courtyard, red-painted timbers, curving roof and a sweeping exterior staircase showing European influence.

8.4 Western Influence

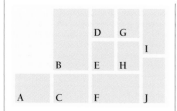

A. German and Italian neoclassical architecture of the 1930s influenced the design of the former Provincial Hall of Ayutthaya, built by a Thai architect in 1941. Columns are topped by sculptures of heroic Ayutthaya kings and queens. Today the hall is a museum.

B. Gothic Revival gone Buddhist: a highlight of Bang Pa-In Palace is the ubosot of Wat Niwetthammaprawat. It was built in 1876 for King Rama V to use in merit-making.

C. Built in 1909, the Royal Thai Army Headquarters is done in neo-Palladian style with a hipped roof and a three-storey verandah.

D. Thailand's grandest avenue, Rachadamnern, was inspired by the Champs-Elysées of Paris. Its central stretch is lined with government buildings done in a modern style in the late 1930s.

E. The Tang Toh Kang Goldshop, built in 1921 from plans by a Dutch architect, is a Chinatown landmark.

F. The mansion of Chao Dara Rasmi, a royal consort of King Rama V, in the Grand Palace's Inner Court.

G. A Victorian-style wooden pavilion, Phlabphla, built in 1896 to serve as a royal railway station near Bang Pa-in Palace.

H. Wat Boworniwet's Phra Tamnak Panya was built by King Rama III as a residence for his brother Prince Mongkut, who served as the temple's abbot before he became king.

I. Bangkok's Thai-Chinese Chamber of Commerce Building was built in 1915 in Renaissance Revival style with Chinese decorative details. It is now a restaurant.

J. The first permanent office of Siam Commercial Bank, founded by a royal prince, was completed in 1908 in Thonburi. It was designed in the Beaux Arts style by Italian architect Annibale Rigotti.

European and colonial architectural influences have been filtering into Thailand since the Ayutthaya period. Western forms have occasionally been cross-bred with Siamese structures, but more often the mixture has been a graft; a Thai roof on a Western structure, European-style rooms within a Thai-style exterior. In other instances, Western architecture has been transplanted wholesale.

The aesthetic peak of Western architectural influence came in the late 19th and early 20th centuries, during the Fourth, Fifth and Sixth Reigns, when the kings built palaces, temples and public buildings in a variety of 19th-century European and colonial styles. This was a conscious effort to assert Siam's modernity and independence in the face of Western colonial expansion in Asia. It also asserted the Chakri dynasty's status vis-a-vis European royalty.

Western materials began to be used in the 19th century: terrazzo, slabs of marble for floors and pavements, glass and stained glass from Belgium and France, and metal fittings for windows and doors. Steel-reinforced concrete construction was introduced. So were structural features such as vaulted ceilings. These new elements allowed buildings to be constructed on a larger scale.

Modernist architecture began to trickle into Thailand in the 1930s and 1940s. More came during the 1950s and 1960s, mostly in the Mid-Century Modern styles popular in the United States, a reflection of both strong American cultural influence in Thailand during the Cold War, and the fact that many Thai architects had studied in the US.

Since the 1960s, architects have worked to fuse local tradition with Western modernism and post-modernism (see Chapter 9, Thai Architectural Forms Today).

8.5 Western-Style Palaces and Mansions

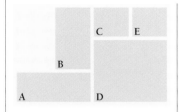

A. *Light and airy, Aphisek Dusit Throne Hall at Dusit Palace is a pinnacle of Thailand's Western-style royal architecture.*

B. *Phayathai Palace was established by King Rama V in 1909. Most of the buildings that remain there, including Phiman Chakri Throne Hall, were completed by King Rama VI in the early 1920s. Done in an eclectic Romantic style, the hall was used for dining and royal audiences.*

C. *Ananta Samakhom Throne Hall, initiated in 1907 by King Rama V, was completed in 1915 by King Rama VI. Its Renaissance-style architecture was designed by a team of Italians. Clad in white Carrara marble, it has six small domes and a large central dome modelled on St Peter's Basilica in Rome.*

D. *Chiang Mai's Daraphirom Palace is an Arts and Crafts-style mansion built by King Rama V's royal consort Princess Dara Rasmi in 1914, a few years after the King's death.*

E. *Tamnak Somdet, the smaller of the two remaining halls at Bang Khun Phrom Palace, was designed in 1913 by German architect Karl Döhring in the Jugendstil fashion.*

Bangkok features a surprisingly broad sampling of authentic 19th-century European architectural styles thanks to the many royal palaces (*wang*), princely residences (*tamnak*) and other mansions built from the mid-19th through to the early 20th centuries. During the Fourth Reign, when these structures first began to be built, they were designed by Thai architects inspired by prints and photographs. King Rama V and his sons hired many European architects to work for the government, a tradition continued in the Sixth Reign. Members of the royal family who were architects also built Western-style structures.

Beyond the buildings constructed or renovated within the Grand Palace compound, each king built secondary palaces around Bangkok and in the provinces, mostly in Western styles. Even more extensive is the collection of royal residences built for the king's sons once they attained the title of prince. These were built large and impressive to serve as places in which the princes could both live and conduct business in their assigned roles as government officials.

After the end of absolute monarchy during the Seventh Reign, the tradition of building princely residences was discontinued, although new royal palaces have been established. Beyond houses for the aristocracy, many other Western-style mansions were built for wealthy Siamese merchants and foreigners living in Siam.

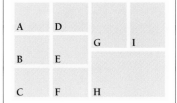

A. The marble staircase in the two-storey central hall of Tamnak Yai at Bang Khun Phrom Palace.

B. King Rama VI's seaside mansion in Phetchburi, Maruekhathayawan Palace, was completed in 1924.

C. Vimanmek Throne Hall at Dusit Palace was more spacious and informal than buildings in the Grand Palace, and became the primary residence for King Rama V and his royal consorts.

D. An interior at Phra Ram Ratchaniwet Palace (Wang Ban Puen) in Phetchburi.

E. The mansion of the lord of Phrae, built in 1892, is decorated with Victorian-style fretwork inside and outside.

F. Another of German architect Karl Döhring's designs is Woradit Palace, built in 1910 as the residence of Prince Damrong Rajanubhab, a historian and archaeologist. Fittings are crafted in the Jugendstil mode, the German counterpart to art nouveau.

G. The king's bathroom at Vimanmek Mansion.

H. Ananta Samakhom Throne Hall, completed in 1915, was the most costly building ever undertaken in Siam up to that time. Done in eclectic late 19th-century Italian style, it featured marble and granite from Italy, metalwork from Stuttgart, Viennese ceramics and tapestries, and draperies and carpets from England. After the end of absolute monarchy, it housed the National Assembly for many years.

I. Royals used the upper floors of their Western-style palaces, while the ground floor was relegated to servants and officials. As a result, the stucco ornament on the second floor of Tamnak Yai at Bang Khun Phrom Palace is more elaborate than on the ground floor.

CHAPTER 9

Thai Architectural Forms Today

From the 1950s through to the 1980s, most of the modernist architecture built in Thailand omitted local references. It is fair to say that as in other countries, too much of it was built without the attention to context, materials, proportions and forms that tend to make for the most pleasing aesthetics. From the late 1980s onwards, however, Thai architects dipped back into their own national design traditions, joining counterparts elsewhere who were reinvigorating modernism with vernacular content. Thailand's most successful results emerged in houses, resorts, museums and temples.

Yet Thailand's tantalisingly rich treasure trove of architectural tradition is not free for the taking. Many of the most aesthetically captivating forms come from religious and royal architecture, which are categories that continue to be held as sacrosanct. The challenge for modern architects is how to work with Thai forms without breaching this hierarchy. Although most palace and temple forms, especially exterior ornament, are considered inappropriate in other buildings, many structural elements and certain underlying concepts are open to reinterpretation. Lessons can be found in floor plans, roof structures, colour schemes, pavilion forms and the proportions of ordination halls. The key is avoiding ostentation and outright mimicry of high architecture.

Traditional architecture of the everyday sort—houses, rice barns, shophouses and so on—is a similarly rich field for modern exploration, with no constraints in terms of reinterpretation. The virtues of this architecture include its adaptation to climate, its deep sense of connection to the local landscape and culture, its suitability to an outdoor lifestyle, its elegant proportions, and the enduring appeal of timber construction. The best Thai-influenced modern buildings allow these and other qualities to shine through, without resorting to sentimentality.

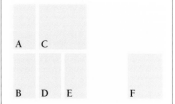

A C

B D E F

A. At Kanchanaburi's Wat Pa Sunantawanaram, the main Buddha image is placed at the centre of the temple under a bamboo trellis.

B. Serving as a gateway to the nearby UNESCO World Heritage Site, Sukhothai Airport makes fitting use of a roof design and brick elements influenced by temple architecture.

C. Yellow paint brightens Baan Rimtai, a house in Chiang Mai.

D. The modern headquarters of the Ministry of Foreign Affairs might be incomplete without traditional guardian figures at the door to ward off evil influences.

E. A modern rendition of a traditional sala serves as a poolside pavilion at Baan Kamonorrathep, a holiday house in Chiang Mai.

F. Plastered balustrades at Baan Rim Tarn, a house in Chiang Mai, make reference to Lanna temple architecture without imitating details.

Preceding pages: Forms drawn from traditional Lanna architecture enhance Baan Rimtai in Chiang Mai. The floor plan is on one level like a traditional house. Wooden elements warm up the reinforced concrete structure. A roof influenced by the multiple tiers of local temples helps ventilation.

9.1 Roof Forms

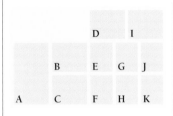

A. A public pavilion at the Rim Tai Saitan residential development in Chiang Mai. The roof loosely reinterprets the pyatthat structure of Burmese-influenced Shan temples. Its rustic simplicity averts a wholesale copying of the sacred roof form.

B. A novel hipped-gable roof with Lanna details distinguishes a Chiang Mai house design by architect M. R. Mitrarun Kasemsri.

C. The relaxed atmosphere of a tropical island resort greets passengers at Samui Airport thanks to the design of its main terminal which takes the form of a pavilion with a hipped, thatched roof. The design is by Habita Architects.

D. The curved roof eaves at Krabi's Tub Kaak resort recall the lines of traditional boats used in the area.

E, G & J. More residential roofs playing on traditional Lanna designs in Chiang Mai's Mae Rim district: Baan Penjati (E), Baan Rimtai (G) and Baan Chang Nag (J).

F. Roofs at Chiang Mai's Tamarind Resort dip low in a style borrowed from Lanna tradition, as designed by architect Ongard Satrabhandhu.

H. The front elevation of Sukhothai Airport reveals both a resemblance to temple architecture and a simplification of traditional design. The design is by Habita Architects.

I. A conference hall at Khon Kaen University features a multi-tiered roof structured after the curving shape of the canopy on a howdah elephant seat.

K. A second eave on the roof of Baan Chom Chan recalls traditional roof structures. The galvanised iron roof tiles in white contrast with trim painted in betel-nut red.

Architects have relied especially on roof forms to give modern buildings a Thai character. Often, they simply borrow the traditional steep gable roof, which offers modern buildings the same practical advantage that it does to traditional Thai houses—efficiently sluicing off rain and ventilating hot air from the interior space below.

Multi-tiered roofs can be used in modern buildings if applied with restraint. Palace- and temple-style ornament— brightly coloured roof tiles and finials such as the *cho fa*—are not considered appropriate on commercial buildings. But multiple tiers, multiple breaks and telescoping roof ends can be adopted for their aesthetic and practical advantages. Because so many modern buildings are large, this traditional approach to roof proportions helps to reduce the appearance of overwhelming size, just as it does in a temple hall. The

breaks between the layers can be used to provide ventilation, as per an ordinary jack roof. Telescoped ends can lend a sense of movement. The roof structure hints at the underlying floor plan of the building, revealing at a glance which end is the entrance. Over a covered stairway, it can follow the descent of steps from the floor level down to the landing, an effect that is elegant and inviting.

Hipped and hipped-gable roofs can also give modern buildings a tropical Asian character, in common with colonial-influenced architecture of Malaysia and Indonesia. These roof forms have become well established in Thailand since they were first used in the 19th century in the construction of royal residences around the country. They have also long been part of Malay-influenced vernacular architecture in Thailand's south, and so they are often used in resorts in such places as Phuket.

9.2 Post-and-Beam Construction

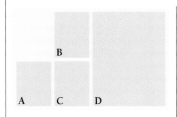

A. The post-and-beam structure lends 'smart casual' style to Baan Pattaya, a beach house.

B. Exposed wooden beams on the gate of Baan Rimtai gives this Chiang Mai house a welcoming air.

C. Masonry columns support wooden beams at a Chiang Mai hotel.

D. Timber posts and beams create an inviting space under the deck at Baan Rimtai.

Traditional post-and-beam construction has many irresistible merits. Unpainted timber takes on an appealing muscularity when it forms a building's exposed structural elements. The post-and-beam approach is an example of an ancient tradition that anticipates modernist precepts about architectural honesty—not hiding structural components behind façades and decoration. Natural limits in the size of timber elements tend to enforce human proportions—a welcome aesthetic. The appropriateness of post-and-beam construction makes it the default approach when building certain types of structures, such as park or garden pavilions.

The scarcity and expense of timber supplies are a constraint, however. Some builders have successfully used post-and-beam construction employing elements made of materials such as reinforced cement instead of wood.

9.3 Buildings Over Water

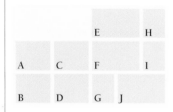

A. At a Chiang Mai vacation house like Baan Kamonorrathep, the swimming pool becomes the heart of the home, around which pavilions and outdoor living spaces are clustered.

B. Architect Chulathat Kitibutr designed Baan Suan restaurant in Chiang Mai to take advantage of spaces by water.

C. A house by architect Kyai Nuipan enjoys a resort-like atmosphere within the heart of Bangkok thanks to an inner courtyard centred on a pool.

D. Baan Hua Hin, a beach house, makes optimal use of a deep, narrow plot by featuring a pool that draws in the ocean views and breeze.

E. At Baan Patong, a holiday house in Phuket, a reflecting pool links the terrace's foreground view to the vista of Patong Bay in the distance. There is no railing to obstruct vision.

F. The cabins of Baan Soi Klang, a house in Bangkok's Sukhumvit district, appear to float over a pool.

G. Baan Bangpli, a house built on a golf course in Samut Prakan.

H. The master bedroom of Rotunda House, near Bangkok, is built as a bridge over a swimming pool in the inner courtyard.

I. Another house that seems to float on water is Baan Kuantrakul, which is divided into two living areas with a connecting level over the pool.

J. A reflecting pool ennobles the headquarters of the Privy Council, the elite group of advisors to the King. Designed by Sumet Jumsai, it stands across from the Grand Palace.

With precedents in both everyday vernacular buildings and the monumental architecture of capitals such as Sukhothai, Ayutthaya and Angkor Wat, pools of water have been used by contemporary architects as elements that transcend landscape design and become integrated with the look and purpose of new Thai buildings. The aesthetic qualities of this approach are clear enough: serenity, coolness, a sense of open space, and the mirroring of the building's image on the water's surface. It promotes breezes around a structure, making it easier to cool the interior using natural ventilation.

The reference within vernacular tradition is to the waterfront houses on stilts seen throughout Thailand. Since ancient times, the local pattern of settlement has followed the course of rivers and seas; villages were always positioned close to water. Modern buildings constructed along dusty roads far from rivers or canals can be symbolically linked to the riparian origins of Thai life by surrounding them with pools of water.

In religious and royal architecture, the significance of water is cosmological—a reference to the oceans surrounding Mount Meru. The moats and basins that enhance the grandeur of Khmer architecture were also employed on a smaller scale in the ancient Thai capitals. Modern institutional buildings such as the chambers of the King's Privy Council (see photo J), allude to this legacy.

9.4 New Thai Houses

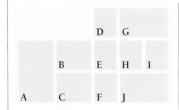

A. *A playful reference to the* naga *balustrades, or nag sadung, of Lanna temple architecture sets the right tone for a weekend home like Baan Rim Tarn in Chiang Mai. An emphasis on the ascent of the stairs prepares guests for the verandah's breathtaking panorama of the surrounding mountains.*

B. *Verdant landscaping and a multi-tiered roof give Baan Chang Nag a Lanna spirit appropriate for Chiang Mai's Mae Rim district.*

C. *As in a traditional Thai house, the area under Baan Pattaya is a multi-purpose room. Here, its purpose is providing a space for relaxation at the beach.*

D. *Architect Kannika Ratanapridakul borrowed Thai forms to achieve practical results at House U3. Three branches of her family needed to fit into one compound, so she created three separate cabins in a U-shaped configuration around a courtyard, like a classic cluster house. She wanted a light-looking roof, and the steep gable form proved ideal.*

E. *A century ahead of its time, Bangkok's Nai Lert House, built in the early 20th century, anticipated today's neo-traditional residential architecture. The multi-tiered, hipped roofs recall Burmese temples.*

F. *At Baan Osataphan in Chiang Mai, a central courtyard leads to indoor/outdoor spaces below the elevated structure of the house.*

G. *Feng shui principles guided the architecture of Baan Sukhumvit 38, a house in Bangkok.*

H & I. *Baan Hua Hin is built on a narrow plot with windows facing an interior courtyard and pool leading towards views of the sea. This format offers privacy while maximising the impact of the seaside vista.*

J. *The terrace adjoining the pool of Baan Kuantrakul functions as an outdoor living room.*

Residential architecture has been a fruitful field for the application of traditional Thai forms. While builders of commercial and institutional projects tend to have narrow constraints, homeowners sometimes have greater freedom to focus on architectural aesthetics. Architects building their own homes have been particularly willing to delve into the use of traditional forms.

One inspiration from the traditional Siamese wooden house is the provision of spaces integrating indoors and outdoors: terraces, verandahs, unenclosed rooms, and open areas underneath a house built on posts. All of these types of structures are being designed into contemporary houses, ideally making use of the traditional tendency to interlink the spaces for greater versatility, so that the hybrid spaces are not isolated but part of a corridor or network of indoor/outdoor 'rooms'.

The exacting proportions of the traditional Siamese house can inspire either emulation or a sense of play. The ratios of roof height to wall heights and widths is one example. Roof features with useful functions, such as *kansaad*-style secondary eaves that shield against the sun and rain, are sometimes adopted. Some references to tradition are simply decorative: trapezoidal windows, for example, and wooden wall panels in the *fa pakon* style.

Beyond houses designed by high-profile architects, tens of thousands of houses built since the 1950s have been constructed using the basic structure of a wooden house on stilts, but the traditional teak wall panels, large terrace and steep concave roof have been replaced with simpler, less expensive components (see 3.1 Gable Roofs, photo F). Often, the owners paint them in cheerful colours such as blue, yellow, green or red, another departure from rigid tradition. These houses are less elegant than the classic versions, but are charming in their own right and easier to adapt to the owner's specific needs, such as in the floor plan.

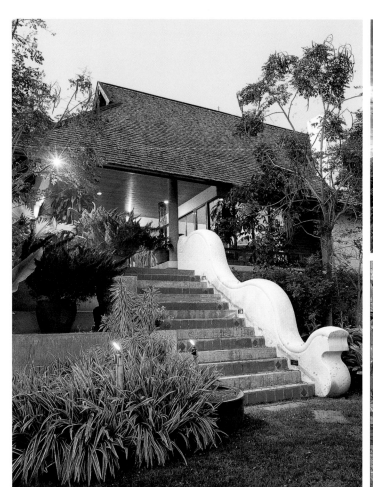

9.5 Jim Thompson's Neo-Traditional House

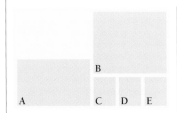

A. *Thompson became Bangkok's top expatriate host by setting up a collection of old timber houses in a verdantly landscaped compound. Exhibitions of contemporary art and traditional textiles are held at a gallery—not shown here—which was built on the site in 2004.*

B. *The international jet set of the 1960s were captivated by the romance of Thompson's antique timber house.*

C. *Thompson transformed the traditional ho nang (sitting room or drawing room) by converting windows into niches for sculptures. Traditional floor cushions were supplanted by rattan furniture.*

D. *Siamese steps traditionally stand outside the house. Enclosing this feature under a roof and between walls gave Thompson a gallery-like space to hang works of art.*

E. *Asian antiques and Thai silk decorate the bedroom and every part of the house.*

By the 1950s, most Thais were inclined to build a Western-style house if they could afford to, preferably of brick and cement. Not, however, Jim Thompson, the expatriate American who helped to revive Thailand's silk industry. In 1958, he bought several teak Thai houses, one dating to the 18th century, transported them to a leafy canal-side spot in Bangkok, and set them up connected with covered walkways to form a palatial compound, the better to display his collection of Southeast Asian antiques and entertain in lavish style. Of hundreds of mansions built by Westerners in Asia, this romantic Siamese house has become the most renowned.

Although it uses traditional components, the house departs from Thai convention. Instead of separate cabins grouped around a central terrace, the cabins are placed in a row, adjoining each other directly or connected by elevated corridors. The house features a dramatic staircase enclosed within the interior, rather than outside steps rising to the terrace. Unlike traditional interiors, rooms are equipped with loose furniture—chairs, tables and cabinets of rattan and lacquered wood, most of them in Chinese style. Instead of a wooden terrace, there is one built of 17th-century bricks from Ayutthaya, encircled by a balustrade of antique Chinese ceramic blocks. The open area below the house is paved with slabs of stone, creating a large covered space for parties.

The result is a new version of the Thai house. Rather than a village home adapted to the practical needs of an extended family, it became an urbane setting for the cosmopolitan social life of a bon vivant. Following Thompson's unexplained disappearance while on holiday in Malaysia's Cameron Highlands in 1967, his assets were used to create a foundation that conserves the house as a museum—one of the region's few traditional-style residences that can be visited by the public.

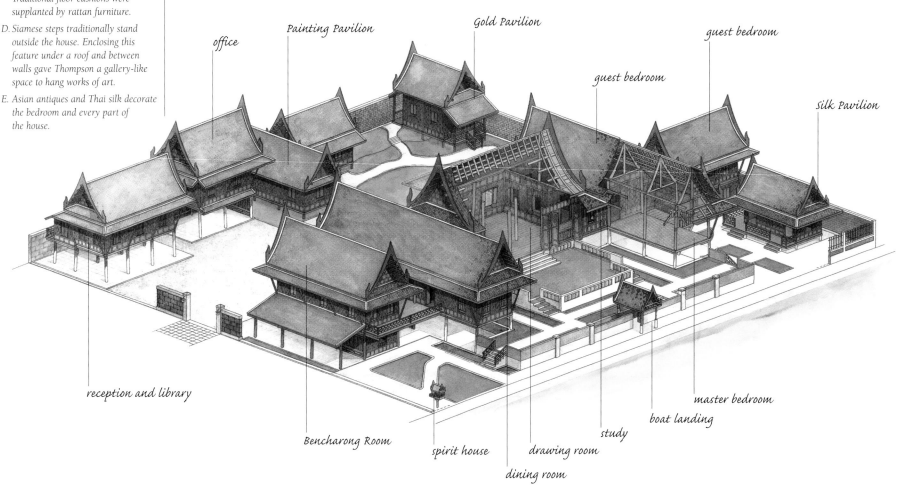

office
Painting Pavilion
Gold Pavilion
guest bedroom
guest bedroom
Silk Pavilion
reception and library
Bencharong Room
spirit house
dining room
drawing room
study
boat landing
master bedroom

9.6 An Artist's Demesne: The Thawan Duchanee House

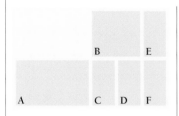

A. *Overlooking a rock garden, this pavilion houses one of the artist's collections of antiques. The roof form is inspired by Laotian-Lanna temple architecture.*

B. *A large hall is created by three adjoining cabins.*

C. *A roof borrows from the graceful proportions and lines of Laotian religious architecture.*

D. *The Farting Pavilion, one of several plaster domes built in a form recalling the chedi. The concave walls of the interior provide ideal acoustics for the farting contests hosted by the artist.*

E. *A shrine-like pavilion that is evocative of a Lanna ho trai.*

F. *A handsome pavilion topped by a hipped roof inspired by Laotian or Tai Lue temples.*

Among the homes built by important artists around the world, perhaps none can surpass Ban Dum Nanglae, the magical compound of some three dozen wooden structures by Thawan Duchanee, one of Asia's best-known painters since his rise to acclaim in the 1970s.

Begun in 1969, this complex of buildings has become larger than many Thai monasteries. Located in Thailand's mountainous, northernmost province of Chiang Rai, where Thawan grew up, the compound is eclectic in its influences, mixing elements from Lanna, Burmese, Laotian, Himalayan, Japanese, Chinese, Indian and Sumatran architecture. It was built by local craftsmen to his designs, while the artist himself crafted such elements as the beautifully carved bargeboard finials. In all these ways, the complex is both innovative and richly Thai.

Thawan has called Ban Dum Nanglae 'a museum for mankind'. Each of the buildings has a different purpose, all shaped more by aesthetic and spiritual intentions than by utility. There is a bird-watching pavilion, art studios, a dome for meditation, and another to house Buddha images. The rock gardens are inspired by Japanese Zen temple courtyards. One stucco dome was built specifically to host the farting contests enjoyed by Thawan's hilltribe neighbours. The walls amplify the smallest sound, adding to the fun of this pungent festival.

The buildings of timber are painted matte black. This has a visual power which recalls Thawan's art, which is mostly done in a monochromatic palette influenced by Chinese and Japanese ink painting and calligraphy. In so many ways, the house is a summation of the artist's life's work.

9.7 A Museum in Neo-Traditional Style: Rai Mae Fah Luang

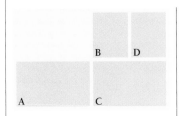

A. *The use of a cruciform mondop structure inspired by religious architecture is appropriate for a public building with a high purpose like this museum.*

B. *Local carpenters proved that traditional Lanna craftsmanship is alive and well today.*

C. *Verdant landscaping, with the inclusion of rare local plants, is part of the museum's attraction.*

D. *The interior of a hall housing royal regalia and other Lanna works of art is cooled naturally by the traditional roof structure with its multiple tiers and ventilation gaps under the eaves.*

When the Mae Fah Luang Foundation's director, Nakorn Pongnoi, set about building a cultural centre in Thailand's northernmost province of Chiang Rai in the 1990s, he decided to give it as much local spirit as possible by hiring craftsmen in the area and allowing the structure to be improvised, rather than commissioning a Bangkok architect. The project's modest budget proved to be an advantage rather than a limitation as the builders put their hearts into it out of affection for the foundation's sponsor, HRH the Princess Mother, the late mother of HM King Bhumibol Adulyadej. The resulting structure has a cruciform floor plan like a Burmese *mondop*, giving the centre an appropriate sense of dignity based on a free interpretation of this local architectural precedent.

HRH the Princess Mother remains one of Thailand's most beloved figures, esteemed for her decades of devotion to public service. From 1988 until her death in 1995, she focused her efforts on creating a rural development project at Chiang Rai's Doi Tung mountain, with the intention of raising living standards and promoting self-sufficiency among the hilltribe people there while restoring the environment and ending the cultivation of opium. The project, which has helped local communities replace economic reliance on opium with new cash crops, high-value handicrafts and tourism, was declared one of the world's most successful alternative development projects by the United Nations.

The project established the park as a centre for studies covering the many ethnic Tai cultures distributed across six nations in Asia. It has also become a popular tourist destination, housing beautiful northern Thai royal regalia and many other artefacts in a large park, which is home to rare indigenous botanical specimens.

9.8 New Religious, Civic and Commercial Buildings

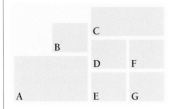

A. *Plain but orderly architecture promotes a tranquil atmosphere suitable for the practice of meditation, the focus of activity at Wat Pa Sunantawanaram. The central pavilion is a multi-purpose hall enshrining a Buddha image, flanked by open pavilions used by monks for prayers, and a courtyard used for walking meditation. Materials are humble: concrete and reclaimed timber.*

B. *At Wat Nong Pah Phong in Ubon Ratchathani, a crematorium for the revered monk Luang Pu Cha was inspired by the form of Isaan chedis in the surrounding province. Instead of an expensive wooden pyre, which wastes wood when it is burned, the temple built a permanent crematorium to use as a chedi memorial tower, with a large interior hall for ceremonies and meditation.*

C. *The headquarters of Thailand's Ministry of Foreign Affairs assumes a diplomatically understated form inspired by the layout of a traditional Siamese cluster house. An inner courtyard contains a lotus pond, a reference to the ministry's emblem, a symbol of purity.*

D. *The Luang Pu Tao Museum, which honours an eminent monk in Nakhon Phanom, features a library for village use on the ground floor. The base, doors and windows are inspired by forms from traditional temples.*

E. *An undecorated chapel at Wat Pa Sunantawanaram enshrines a single Buddha image, reflecting the temple's precept of simplicity.*

F. *The United Nations Conference Centre makes reference to the overlapping roof forms that characterise Asian architecture.*

G. *A meditation pavilion at Phayao's Wat Analayo is built over a cliff with dramatic views of the forest and mountains. This scenery forms an inspiring backdrop for a Buddha image at one end of the sala.*

Traditional forms have been a wellspring of inspiration for new sacred and public architecture. The size and function of many of these buildings encourage architects to adapt features from traditional religious and royal style that would be inappropriate in a residential application. Commercial architecture too can successfully draw on these traditions if they are approached with sensitivity.

Interesting results have emerged in the construction of new temples. Most of this innovation has been sponsored by religious institutions outside the mainstream—alternative Buddhist sects and so-called 'forest' temples. *Wats* governed by the central Sangha Council must follow relatively strict guidelines on form and decoration set by the government's Department of Religious Affairs.

Within these guidelines, conventional temples tend to be built with ever more ornate decoration, reflecting the wish of lay people to make merit by donating funds for construction. The alternative temples have instead tended towards restraint and simplicity. The underlying structure and purpose of a Buddhist temple is combined with the pared down aesthetics of modernism to create spaces conducive to meditation.

New civic buildings such as museums, university halls and government offices have started to show friendlier modern faces by adapting Siamese elements including pools, multi-tiered roofs and the use of an elevated structure on posts. Some new hotels feature temple-style courtyard layouts.

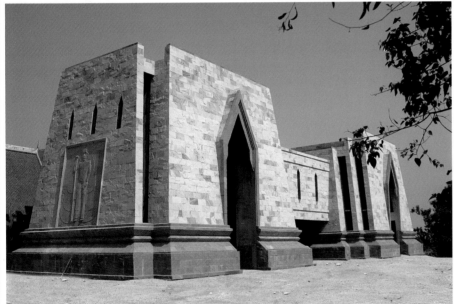

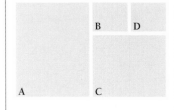

A. Designed by Ongard Satrabhandhu, the Tamarind Village Hotel in Chiang Mai is laid out like a temple cloister with a courtyard centring on a beautiful old tamarind tree.

B. Pavilions at Mae Fah Luang Museum in Chiang Rai combine plastered columns, wood-shingled roofs and open-air verandah spaces in a manner recalling local temple architecture.

C. Rajamankha Hotel in Chiang Mai borrows roof forms from Lanna temple style. As designed by Ongard Satrabhandhu, the hotel's courtyard layout displays the architecture splendidly.

D. The design of the Phuket Museum quotes from the traditional structure of southern houses. The wooden gable panel was inspired by old-fashioned gables woven from bamboo. It was designed by architect Udom Sakulpanich in 1986.

Map of Thailand

Places of architectural interest

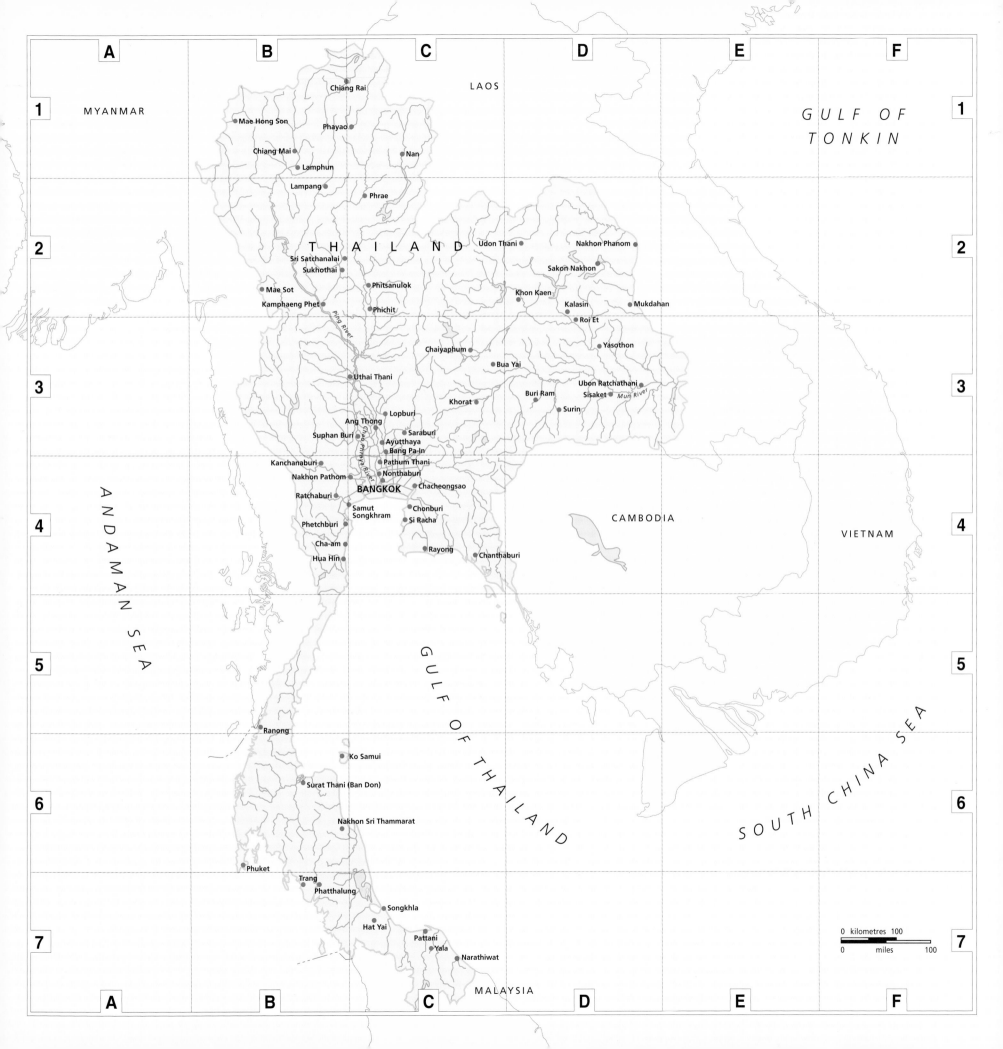

Glossary and Chronology

Ayutthaya
capital of Siam, 1351–1767, and the name of this historical era; today it is a province and heritage site.

baan rim naam
house built on posts near or directly above a waterway.

bai
leaves.

bai raka
fin-like projections on a temple roof windbreak or bargeboard, suggesting fins of *naga*, feathers of *garuda* or both.

bai sema or bai sima
the eight boundary markers around the *ubosot*, designating a temple's sacred grounds for monks' ceremonies.

ban talaeng
Thai-style decorative arch used over temple and palace windows and doors in the form of an ornamented gable.

blanor
hipped-gable roof. Also known as Manila or gambrel roof.

Bo or Bodhi tree
sacred tree under which the Buddha meditated and found enlightenment.

bodhisatta
Pali term for one of the 550 Buddhas-to-be of the Jataka tales, in Theravada Buddhism.

bodhisattva
Sanskrit term for someone destined for Buddha-hood who postpones enlightenment to save others, in Mahayana Buddhism.

Brahma
the god of creation in the main trinity of Hindu deities; depicted with four faces (*phra phrom* in Thai).

Brahmanism
ancient Indian religion which evolved into Hinduism and Buddhism.

busabok
spire-roofed altar, pulpit or throne in the form of a Hindu aerial chariot.

chaan
terrace or deck of a Siamese house on posts.

chang sip moo
the ten crafts; traditional artisan guilds that practiced architectural and other crafts.

chedi
a memorial tower, usually bell-shaped, enshrining ashes of the Buddha or other sacred relics.

cho fa
sky tassle; sacred guardian finial on the apex of a palace or temple roof.

deva
Sanskrit or Pali for a divinity or angel; known as *thep, thewa* or *thewada* in Thai.

devaraja
Sanskrit term referring to the concept of the 'divine king', derived from Hindu-Khmer culture.

dhamma
Buddhist doctrine or law.

dhammachakra
Wheel of the Law; a carved stone sculpture of a wheel representing the doctrine of Buddhism.

dhammaraja
the concept of the moral king who is viewed as a *boddhisattva* and who rules according to the righteous precepts of Buddhism, derived from Khmer Mahayana culture.

Dhammayuthika
Pali term for reformist Theravada Buddhist sect founded in the 19th century by King Rama IV.

Erawan
white elephant divinity that serves as Indra's mount and has many heads; in Thai architecture it is usually depicted with three heads.

fa pakon
pre-assembled wooden wall panel of a house; its boards are constructed in a grid pattern of tall rectangles.

Garuda
Hindu god who is half-man, half-bird and serves as the vehicle of Narai; other lesser *garudas* also inhabit the celestial realm.

Hamsa
sacred goose that is the mount of Brahma; Buddhist symbol of purity and enlightenment (*hong* or *hongse* in Thai).

ham yom
sacred testicles; carved wooden guardian plaque over the door of a bedroom in a Lanna house.

hang hong
goose tail; the upturned finial on the lower end of a temple or palace barge-board, often in the form of a *naga* head.

hang pla
fish tail; lower finial of a house wind-break styled in the form of a fish's tail.

harmika
Sanskrit term for the rectangular platform between the dome and spire of a *chedi*, symbolising Buddha's throne.

Himaphan
mythical Hindu-Buddhist paradise in the Himalayas populated by myriad fantastical creatures.

ho
house, palace, hall or pavilion.

ho chaek
Isaan term for sermon hall, or *sala kan parian*.

ho khrua
house cabin used as a kitchen.

ho klang
an open pavilion in a large Siamese cluster house.

ho nang
cabin or open pavilion used as a sitting room in a Siamese house.

ho rakhang
belfry of a Buddhist temple.

ho trai
scripture pavilion for storage of sacred Buddhist manuscripts (*ho thamma* in Lanna).

Indra
ruler of the Hindu gods and Mount Meru; a protector of Buddha.

Jataka
morally instructive tales of the Buddha's life or past lives, often depicted in temple murals.

kala
guardian figure with a demonic, mask-like face.

kalae
V- or X-shaped wooden decoration extending from the gable-end peaks of a Lanna house, thought to represent the horns of the water buffalo.

kampaeng kaew
emerald walls; special walls enclosing inner courtyards of *wats* and palaces.

kansaad
the long, secondary or lower eave of a house roof, usually supported by brackets or posts.

khan thuai
wood or plaster brackets supporting roof eaves, usually of a temple or palace.

khao more
Chinese-influenced stone mountain representing Mount Meru and the afterlife, used to decorate courtyards and gardens.

khruang muk
mother-of-pearl inlay, often used to ornament doors and windows.

kinnara (male), **kinnaree** (female)
mythical half-bird, half-human Himaphan creature.

kong khiew
eyebrow-shaped decorative arch under temple gables and door lintels.

kranok
Siamese decorative motifs in forms suggesting stylised flowers, flames and leaves.

kranok karn khot
kranok motifs arranged in a vine-like, coiling pattern.

ku
gilded shrine enclosing a Buddha image inside a Lanna *viharn*.

kuti
monks' cabins.

lamyong
decorations on the windbreak on the gable end of a palace or temple roof (corresponding to the *panlom* of a house); usually ornamented with gilding or glass mosaic, it has carvings and finials in the form of guardian figures such as *naga, garuda, makara* or *hamsa*.

luk nimit
sacred spheres usually made of stone, which are buried under *bai sema* to consecrate the grounds of an *ubosot*.

maha monthian
the king's residential halls in the Grand Palace.

maha prasat
ceremonial throne halls in the Grand Palace topped by a seven-tiered spire.

Mahayana Buddhism
the form of Buddhism practiced in China, Tibet, Japan and Korea that emphasises the role of *bodhisattvas* in salvation; sometimes practiced in Thailand, Cambodia and Burma.

mai dat
the Siamese art of bonsai gardening.

makara
mythical beast like a crocodile, often with a dolphin's body and elephant's trunk (*man kan* in Thai); appears as a *wat* guardian figure on roofs and balustrades.

Mara
evil demon of desires who tried to tempt the Buddha away from enlightenment.

mek lai
'floating cloud' motif of Chinese origin, from Indian antecedents.

meru
crematorium (*men* in Thai), derived from Mount Meru.

mondop
structural form with a square floor plan and spired or pyramidal roof, often used as a reliquary, *ho trai* or *ho rakhang*.

mongkut
Siamese crown and also a form of *wat* roof spire of circular diminishing tiers representing Mount Meru. Also the name of King Rama IV.

Mount Meru
mythical mountain of 33 tiers at the centre of the universe in Hindu cosmology.

naa ban
decorated triangular gable end or pediment of a temple or palace.

naa chua
the triangular gable end or pediment of a house.

naatang
window.

naga
Sanskrit or Pali for mythical water serpents (*naak* in Thai), often *wat* guardian figures on balustrades, eave brackets and roof finials.

nak lamyong
naga body decoration on a temple or palace windbreak.

nak sadung
Khmer-influenced balustrade or *lamyong* in the form of a *naga*.

Narai
incarnation of Vishnu; one of three gods of the main Hindu trinity, usually depicted on his mount Garuda. He is a symbol of the Thai king, who is considered an incarnation of Rama, who in turn is an incarnation of Vishnu.

ngao
horn-like finial on a house *panlom*, probably derived from a *naga* figure.

nophasun
nine-pronged finial representing the thunderbolt (*vajra*) of Indra or Siva atop a *prang*. Also called *fak pega*.

Pali
ancient southern Indian scriptural language of Theravada Buddhism.

panlom
bargeboard or windbreak on the gable of a house roof protecting the tiles or thatch from the weather.

panya
hipped roof; known as *lima* in the south.

phra
honorific, meaning 'Lord' or 'Venerable'.

phra kaew morakot
Emerald Buddha; Thailand's most sacred Buddha image and the Palladium of State.

phra merumas
royal crematorium built of wood for temporary ceremonial use. See also *meru*.

phra that
a *chedi* of highest importance enshrining a Buddha relic.

phutthawat
walled ceremonial or sacred zone of a *wat*, enclosing the *viharn*, *ubosot*, etc.

prang
Khmer or Khmer-influenced Hindu sanctuary or Buddhist memorial tower with a bullet-shaped top.

prasat
cruciform palace throne hall with a five-tiered roof spire.

purnaghata
Sanskrit term for ancient Buddhist icon of an ever-blooming pot of flowers.

pyatthat
Burmese-style multi-tiered temple roof.

rabiang khot or *phra rabiang*
cloisters or roofed gallery enclosing the inner temple courtyard.

Rama
incarnation of Vishnu, symbol of the perfect king.

Ramakian
Thai rendition of the ancient Hindu epic about the adventures of Rama, the Ramayana.

ran kha rim tang
roadside kiosk, shed or pavilion used to vend such products as fruit, vegetables, handicrafts or packaged goods.

ran ruen
A Thai-style shop or shophouse used for both living and trade, traditionally built of timber on one storey.

Rattanakosin
short for the official Thai name of Bangkok. Also names the current era of Thai history which began with King Rama I's founding of Bangkok as Siam's new capital in 1782 and the commencement of the Chakri dynasty's reign.

ruen khrueng phook
house of bamboo.

ruen pae
raft house; usually a gable-roofed cabin built on wood, bamboo or metal pontoons.

sala
Pali term for pavilion.

sala kan parian
Pali term for study hall or sermon hall in a *wat*, where monks instruct lay people; called a *ho chaek* in Isaan.

sanam luang
Royal Field; the open field or park in front of the Grand Palace, used for royal ceremonies such as cremations. Also called *thung phra men*, or royal cremation grounds.

sangha
Pali term for Buddhist clergy of ordained monks and novices.

sanghawat
Pali term for the residential zone of a *wat* compound containing monks' cabins, or *kuti*, and other monastic facilities.

san phra phum
miniature house or shrine for a guardian spirit or deity.

Sanskrit
ancient Indian scriptural language of Mahayana Buddhism; used in some Khmer and Thai inscriptions.

sao
post, column or pillar.

Shan
a Tai ethnic group also known as Tai Yai, centred in northern Burma and northern Thailand.

Siam
name of the Thai nation, particularly the Ayutthaya, Thonburi and Rattanakosin kingdoms, before it was renamed Prathet Thai, or Thailand, in 1939. The term 'Siamese' is used loosely in this book to refer to the architecture, culture and people of the central region from the 13th through to the early 20th centuries.

singha
mythical lion, often a *wat* guardian figure, especially in the north (*singh* in Thai).

Srivijaya
ancient kingdom centred in Indonesia and the Malay peninsula from the 8th to the 13th centuries.

Sukhothai
name of the major early Siamese kingdom founded around 1238 and absorbed into Ayutthaya in 1378; today it is a province and heritage site. Also the name given to this period, considered the first era of Thai history.

Tai
the transnational group of peoples that includes the Thais, Laotians, Shans, Tai Lue and others in China, Southeast Asia and northeast India.

Tai Lue
a Tai ethnic group that has migrated to northern Thailand from Sipsongphanna in southern China.

tamnak
the palace of a prince.

theng na or *thieng na*
field hut, pavilion or cabin built for temporary shelter in rice fields located far from the village.

theppanom
an angel or divinity (*thep*) in a pose of prayer or adoration.

Theravada
Doctrine of the Elders; the conservative form of Buddhism practiced in Thailand, Southeast Asia and Sri Lanka.

thewada
see *deva*.

Thonburi
area west of the Chao Phraya River that served as the capital of Siam from 1767 to 1782 under King Taksin; it is now part of Bangkok. Also the name of that kingdom and period.

Traiphum
The Three Worlds; Thai treatise on Hindu-Buddhist cosmology describing heaven, hell and earth (Traibhumi in Thai).

Tripitaka
The Three Baskets; main scriptures of Theravada Buddhism.

ubosot or *bot*
ordination hall (a *sim* in Isaan), or Buddhist chapel where monks are ordained; stands on sacred ground marked by *bai sema*.

vajra
Sanskrit term for the lightning bolt of Hindu gods Indra and Siva, depicted as a double trident atop *prangs*. See also *nophasun*.

viharn
assembly hall, or Buddhist chapel, that houses Buddha images and murals, used for ceremonies involving both monks and lay people.

wang
the royal palace of a king; the Grand Palace is the *wang luang*.

wat
Buddhist temple or monastery. Also commonly used to designate Hindu, Christian and Muslim worship sites.

yak
mythical giants often embodied in *wat* guardian figures.

yong
carved wooden panels that decorate the exterior base of windows in Siamese timber houses.

yoong khao or *yong khao*
rice barn or granary (*long khao* or *ye khao* in the north).

Thai History and Prehistory (Major Kingdoms)			
Dvaravati (Mon)	6th–9th centuries	Lanna	13th–18th centuries
Lopburi (Khmer)	9th–13th centuries	Ayutthaya	1351–1767
Srivijaya	8th–13th centuries	Thonburi	1767–1782
Sukhothai	13th–15th centuries	Rattanakosin	1782–present

Chakri Dynasty Kings (Rattanakosin Era)	
First Reign	King Rama I, Phra Phutthayotfa (1782–1809)
Second Reign	King Rama II, Phra Phutthaloetla (1809–1824)
Third Reign	King Rama III, Phra Nangklao (1824–1851)
Fourth Reign	King Rama IV, Mongkut (1851–1868)
Fifth Reign	King Rama V, Chulalongkorn (1868–1910)
Sixth Reign	King Rama VI, Vajiravudh (1910–1925)
Seventh Reign	King Rama VII, Prajadhipok (1925–1935)
Eighth Reign	King Rama VIII, Ananda Mahidol (1935–1946)
Ninth Reign	King Rama IX, Bhumibol Adulyadej (1946–present)

Picture Credits

252

References

Aasen, Clarence T., *Architecture of Siam: A Cultural History Interpretation*, Oxford University Press, Kuala Lumpur, 1998.

Apinan Poshyananda, *Modern Art in Thailand: Nineteenth and Twentieth Centuries*, Oxford University Press, Singapore, 1992.

Brezeale, Kennon, *From Japan to Arabia: Ayutthaya's Maritime Relations with Asia*, White Lotus Co., Bangkok, 2001.

Chami Jotisalikorn, Tettoni, Luca Invernizzi, Phuthorn Bhumidon and McKeen Di Crocco, Virginia, *Classic Thai: Design, Interiors, Architecture*, Periplus, Singapore, 1999.

Cornwel-Smith, Philip and Goss, John, *Very Thai: Everyday Popular Culture*, River Books, Bangkok, 2005.

Cushman, Richard D. (translator), *The Royal Chronicles of Ayutthaya*, The Siam Society, Bangkok, 2000.

Dumarcay, Jacques, *The House in South-East Asia*, Oxford University Press, London, 1987.

Freeman, Michael, *Lanna: Thailand's Northern Kingdom*, River Books, Bangkok, 2001.

Garnier, Derick, *Ayutthaya: Venice of the East*, River Books, Bangkok, 2004.

Gerini, G. E., *Siam and Its Productions, Arts, and Manufactures (1911)*, White Lotus Co., Bangkok, 2001.

Gilquin, Michel and Smithies, Michael (translator), *The Muslims of Thailand*, IRASEC and Silkworm Books, Chiang Mai, 2005.

Gosling, Betty, *Origins of Thai Art*, River Books, Bangkok, 2004.

Graham, Mark, *Thai Wood*, Finance One Public Co., Bangkok, 1996.

Hasan-Uddin Khan, *Contemporary Asian Architects*, Taschen, Cologne, 1995.

Hope, Ryan, Hope, Kate and Hope, Elize (eds.), *The Master Architects Series V: Architects 49 Selected and Current Works*, Images Publishing Group, Australia, 2002.

Hoskin, John, *Bangkok by Design: Architectural Diversity in the City of Angels*, Art Data, Bangkok, 1995.

Joti Kalyanamitra, *Dictionary of Thai Architecture*, Office of the National Culture Commission, Bangkok, 1993.

———, *Six Hundred Years of Work by Thai Artists & Architects*, Association of Siamese Architects, Bangkok, 2003.

Matics, K. I., *Introduction to the Thai Temple*, White Lotus, Bangkok, 1992.

McGill, Forrest and M. L. Pattaratorn Chirapravati, *The Kingdom of Siam: The Art of Central Thailand, 1350–1800*, Art Media Resources, Chicago, 2005.

Montgomery, Jock and Warren, William, *Menam Chao Phraya: River of Life & Legend*, Post Books, Bangkok, 1994.

Moore, Elizabeth, Suriyavudh Sukvasti, Freeman, Michael and Stott, Phillip, *Ancient Capitals of Thailand*, River Books, Bangkok, 1996.

Munro-Hay, Stuart, *Nakhon Sri Thammarat: The Archaeology, History and Legend of a Southern Thai Town*, White Lotus Press, Bangkok, 2002.

Naengnoi Punjabhan, Aroonrut Wichienkeeo and Somchai na Nakhonphanom, *The Charm of Lanna Wood Carving*, Rerngrom Pub. Co., Bangkok 1994.

Naengnoi Punjabhan and Somchai na Nakhonphanom, *The Art of Thai Wood Carving: Sukhothai, Ayutthaya, Rattanakosin*, Rerngrom Pub. Co., Bangkok, 1993.

———, *The Soul of Isan Wood Carving*, Rerngrom Pub. Co, Bangkok, 1993.

Naengnoi Suksri and Freeman, Michael, *The Grand Palace*, River Books, Bangkok, 1999.

———, *Palaces of Bangkok: Royal Residences of the Chakri Dynasty*, River Books, Bangkok, 1996.

Pan, Lynn (ed.), *The Encyclopedia of the Chinese Overseas*, Archipelago Press/Landmark Books, Singapore, 1998.

Pasuk Phongpaichit and Baker, Chris, *A History of Thailand*, Cambridge, 2005.

———, *Thailand: Economy and Politics*, Oxford University Press, Oxford, 1995.

Peleggi, Maurizio, *Lords of Things: The Fashioning of the Siamese Monarchy's Modern Image*, Bangkok, University of Hawaii Press, Honolulu, 2002.

Ping Amranand, *Andaman Style*, Amulet Production, Bangkok, 2002.

Ping Amranand and Warren, William, *Lanna Style: Art & Design of Northern Thailand*, Monsoon Editions, Bangkok, 2000.

Pisit Charoenwong (ed.), *The Sights of Rattanakosin*, The Fine Arts Department, Bangkok, 1982.

Pongkwan Sukwattana Lassus (ed.), *Architectural Heritage in Thailand*, Association of Siamese Architects, Bangkok, 2004.

Powell, Robert, *The New Thai House*, Select Publishing, Singapore, 2003.

Reid, Anthony, *Charting the Shape of Early Modern Southeast Asia*, Silkworm Books, Chiang Mai, 2000.

Ringis, Rita, *Thai Temples and Temple Murals*, Oxford University Press, Kuala Lumpur, 1990.

Ruethai Chaichongrak, Somchai Nil-athi, Ornsiri Panin, Saowalak Posayanonda and Freeman, Michael, *Thai House*, River Books, Bangkok 2002.

Santi Leksukhum, *Temples of Gold*, River Books, Bangkok, 2000.

Silpa Bhirasri, *Thai Wood Carvings*, The Fine Arts Department, Bangkok, 1961.

Smitthi Siribhadra, Moore, Elizabeth and Freeman, Michael, *Palaces of the Gods: Khmer Art & Architecture in Thailand*, River Books, Bangkok, 1997.

Sompop Piromya, Vivat Temiyabandha, Khate Ratanajarana and Wiroj Srisuro, *Thai Houses*, Mutual Fund Public Co., Bangkok, 1995.

Sumet Jumsai, *Naga: Cultural Origins in Siam and the West Pacific*, Oxford University Press, Singapore, 1990.

Tanistha Dansilp and Freeman, Michael, *Things Thai*, Periplus, Hong Kong, 2002.

Tettoni, Luca Invernizzi, *Chiang Mai and Northern Thailand*, Asia Books, Bangkok, 1992.

Van Beek, Steve, *Arts of Thailand*, Thames & Hudson, London, 1985.

———, *Bangkok Then and Now*, AB Publications, Bangkok, 2000.

Van De Cruysse, Dirk and Smithies, Michael, *Siam and the West, 1500–1700*, Silkworm Books, Chiang Mai, 2002.

Warren, William, Beurdeley, Jean-Michel and Tettoni, Luca Invernizzi, *Jim Thompson: The House on the Klong*, Archipelago Press, Singapore, 1999.

Waterson, Roxana, *The Living House: An Anthropology of Architecture in South East Asia*, Thames & Hudson Ltd, Singapore, 1997.

Winichakul Thongchai, *Siam Mapped: A History of the Geo-body of a Nation*, Silkworm Books, Chiang Mai, 1994.

Wyatt, David K., *Thailand: A Short History*, Yale University Press, New Haven, 1984.

Index

Note: Page numbers in *italic* refer to illustrations.